DRIVEN TO THE EDGE

DRIVEN TO THE EDGE

A Biblical Examination of Suicide

By

Randy Raynes

SWORD of the LORD
PUBLISHERS

P. O. Box 1099, Murfreesboro, TN 37133

Printed and Bound in the United States of America

DEDICATION

As I think of the subject of suicide and those affected by it, I am reminded of how truly blessed I have been. The Lord has brought several people into my life who have been an encouragement and help in times of need. This book is dedicated to three of those people.

The first is my dad, Jess Howard. Because of his sacrifice and hard work I was able to finish college, enter the ministry and serve the Lord. There are many things a father goes through for his children that are never noticed and appreciated until his children have children of their own. I have grown to love and appreciate Dad more than he will ever know.

Another person who has played an important role in my life is Lester Robertson. He was my Sunday school teacher when I was a teenager, my friend and like a second father to me. He was always there when I needed a friend and was a real encouragement every time I saw him. I have missed him since the Lord has taken him home to Heaven.

A third person who has been a tremendous help since I entered the ministry is my own pastor, Jim Chase. He has been a guide to me through the difficulties of the ministry. I have found him to be more than just a pastor: he is also a dear friend. My family and I have found him to be a source of encouragement and wisdom as we have faced the trials of life in the ministry.

Many people desperately need someone to show them what these men have shown me. My prayer is that I can be to people what these men have been to me.

Randy Raynes

CONTENTS

FOREWORD

One of the many opportunities I have had since becoming a pastor was to be an assistant to the chaplain of the New Hanover County Sheriff's Department in Wilmington, North Carolina. One of the many things we were called upon to do was to deal with inmates who were considered suicidal. It was while serving in this capacity that I began to realize that there are many people who are hurting for various reasons and the stock answers that we have learned to give out so quickly do not always work as we would like. It is easy to tell someone just to trust the Lord and everything will turn out all right. However, to a person who has reached rock bottom, that answer many times offers very little comfort. When this person is a viable candidate for suicide, we realize that we need more than just a simple answer. We become acutely aware of the fact that what we say to this person had better have more power and authority than our own personal beliefs.

People want something on which to rest all their hopes and aspirations. This book is written for the purpose of presenting biblical answers to both the suicidal and to those suffering the aftermath of suicide.

I realize that of the many who commit suicide, some do so as a result of the side effects of mental illness and/or the use of prescription drugs. This book is not designed to deal with these but with people who willfully and intellectually choose suicide. The answers in this book are designed to be given to those of rational thought.

I realize that I do not have all the answers, nor do I consider myself an expert on human nature. I do know, however, that the Lord has the answers and that the Bible is the Book the Lord has given us to use in dealing with the problems of life. I do not attempt to present to you what I think but rather what the Lord tells us in His Word. It is my hope and desire that in doing so, this book will be of help to all who read it.

INTRODUCTION

It's the middle of the night, and the phone rings. The voice at the other end of the line is that of a distraught man, desperately needing to talk to someone.

"Pastor, I'm sorry to bother you at this time, but I don't know what to do. I've tried to tell myself it is going to be all right, but I don't think I can live any longer. I'm thinking about committing suicide, but I know that would be wrong. Can you help me?"

Immediately you ask the Lord to give you enough wisdom to help this individual.

* * *

The phone rings. "Pastor, I have a friend who has been going through some really difficult problems. I'm afraid he is suicidal. He has agreed to talk to you. Can you go by and see him?"

Again anxiety starts to build. You realize someone is looking for wisdom and answers you do not have. Again you find yourself praying and asking God to help you as you deal with this person.

* * *

Suicide is a subject most people would rather not talk about. But sadly, the number of cases of suicide has been on the increase, especially among those who are ill and also among teenagers.

On January 13, 1997, a morning news program reported the findings of a survey taken among ninth graders. Forty-three percent of the students surveyed said they knew someone who had committed suicide.

One does not have to go far to find someone who has attempted, or is thinking of attempting, such an act. Even among Christians suicide is far more common than we would like to imagine. I have heard of suicide among those in all walks of life. Even if you do not now know of someone who has committed suicide, chances are that you will.

I am amazed at the ideas people have regarding suicide. I have heard statements such as "You cannot go to Heaven if you commit suicide," or, "He or she must not have been a Christian." These remarks are usually made by those who have not lost a loved one to suicide. Those mourning the suicide of a friend or loved one seem more concerned with finding answers to help them deal with their grief and guilt, than they are with condemning their loved one.

My purpose in writing this book is threefold:

(1) To help those who are seriously contemplating suicide. I want to give some solid reasons why no one should choose to end his life. These reasons will not be what I think but what the Lord has to say about it.

(2) To help those who carry a heavy load of guilt. Untold numbers are suffering from the suicide of someone they knew. Right now they look at the situation and try to find comfort but find none. They plague themselves with the "what if's." I trust I will give such people some insight as to why their loved one would do such a deed, then give some thoughts from the Bible that offer comfort.

(3) To help those dealing with persons who are contemplating suicide. We never know how close we are to those who consider it a viable option, so we need to be ready to give them an answer.

As I began my study, I was amazed at how many people thought the subject of suicide was foreign to the Bible. Some viewed it as a strange subject for a Bible study. As I read through the Bible, I found more than a little on the subject.

My prayer is that you, the reader, will find help and comfort.

Chapter 1

WHY A BOOK ON SUICIDE?

The first thing to consider is the necessity for such a book. Why should one write a book on such a subject? Suicide has become very prominent in our society. There are very few people who do not know someone who has at least attempted it. When I have preached on this subject of suicide, I have asked for a show of hands of those who know someone who has attempted suicide. It is amazing how many hands go up. There is a great chance that you yourself know such a one.

I am reminded of my first experience in dealing with the suicide of someone I knew. When I was in my middle teens, a young boy named Jimmy, also a teenager, attended my home church. Not very many children liked Jimmy because he was always getting into trouble. Besides being a bully to the smaller kids, he was a pest to the older ones and a bother to the adults.

During one week of revival meetings at our church, Jimmy went forward every night during the invitation. He would tell the pastor that he wanted to be saved. That first night most people were excited. They thought salvation was what this boy needed; but when he continued coming forward each night, people became annoyed.

Some time later Jimmy and his family moved to another town, thus ending our experiences with him.

One day we received word that Jimmy had taken his dad's gun and killed himself. We were all shocked, and many were ashamed as they thought of how they had treated him. The guilt that some felt was obvious. Questions soon followed: "Could we have done something to help?" "Was he asking for help when he kept coming forward during the revival?" "Could we be partly to blame?"

I am reminded of an inmate in the New Hanover County Jail. He had already spent time in prison for a murder he had committed; he was again in jail, accused of a double murder. We spent several minutes every Sunday in his cell block trying to help him but were unsuccessful. He told us it was too late for him and to spend our time trying to reach others before they followed the path he had taken.

Found guilty of kidnapping, he was sentenced to life in prison. Then he was transferred to a neighboring county to face double-murder charges.

A few months later we heard on the news that on the day of his sentencing, he was found hanging in his cell. He had decided, after having been found guilty of double murder, he would end the whole ordeal by committing suicide.

I know of a pastor who took a gun and shot himself while sitting in the church office. I know a young man who found his best friend with a knife in his chest. Yesterday I was told of someone else who had committed suicide.

A doctor who had once sworn to help heal started a doctor-assisted suicide practice, all in the name of mercy. His whole defense is that he is just trying to help ease the pain of the patient. We used to have doctors who tried to convince people of the value of life and the need to live. But thanks to today's liberal thinking, we have taken the value of life out of people's thinking. We have declared that a life of pain has no value. The next step is to say that the life of the severely retarded has no redeeming value. We are becoming a society of people who stand at the foot of a building and yell, "Jump!" to the man standing on the edge.

What "Dr. Death" is doing is no different than what a teenager by the name of James did in Wilmington, North Carolina. James' friend had broken up with his girlfriend. His friend had no desire to live if it meant living without her. Not having the courage to kill himself, he paid James fifty dollars to do the job for him.

James took the fifty dollars, with no intention of killing his friend. His friend kept prodding him until James took a knife and stabbed him in the chest. The last I heard, James was still serving a life sentence in the North Carolina prison system.

I ask you, What is the difference between what he did once and what "Dr. Death" has done many times and still continues to do?

Some would say the difference is in the *reason* for the suicide. Some would say that we cannot compare the emotional pain of breaking up with a girlfriend to the physical pain of a terminal illness. However, the pain of the teenager in Wilmington was just as real to him as any pain felt by those who have chosen to end their lives at the hands of "Dr. Death."

Many might think the difference is *greed*. They would say that James did it for the money. Fifty dollars is a small sum for which to end someone's life. But if you think the difference is money, think again.

I cannot say whether "Dr. Death" has been paid for his services, but if our government puts its approval on "doctor-assisted suicide," it will not come free of charge. It will be just another chapter in the doctrine of death which is being promoted today. First is abortion, the killing of the unborn; second, doctor-assisted suicide, the killing of the ill; next may be the genocide of the severely retarded, the disabled, the elderly and anyone else not deemed beneficial to our society.

Today the reason is medical; tomorrow, emotional; after that, for any reason. Before long, the promoters of suicide will be calling it "everyone's constitutional right to die."

One sad aspect of this whole affair is the attitude many have developed concerning this subject. Just go to a barber shop or any other public place and listen to the talk concerning suicide. The propaganda of those promoting death has spread throughout our society. So many people place such little value on the life given to them.

Many say it is only *humane* to help someone who is sick end his life, but the Bible teaches us that it is ungodly. Many say that man has a right to choose when he wants to die, but the Bible teaches that God breathed into man the breath of life, thus making him a living soul. God gave life to each individual for a purpose, and no individual has a right to tell God when his life needs to end.

Have we forgotten God and His will? Have we forgotten just who is supposed to be in control? I believe even a life of pain has value and purpose. The value is God-given and should be "God-taken."

For every suicide there are those left behind who must deal with the aftermath.

I was recently told of a man who was having to deal with the suicide of his teenage daughter. I talked with a man whose wife was having trouble dealing with the suicide of her best friend. Parents, children, husbands, wives, friends, relatives—all have to deal with the aftermath of suicide. They all ask the same questions: *"Why did he/she do it?"*

"Could I have done anything to have prevented it?"
"Shouldn't I have done something about it?"

The end result of suicide is guilt, broken hearts and years of pain and shame.

I know of a man whose father committed suicide several years ago, and this man is still suffering from it. How painful it is to have to tell someone that his loved one died at his own hand.

The American Heritage Dictionary defines *suicide* as "the act of, or instance of, killing oneself." It is self-murder, the act of destroying one's own life. One quote I read put it this way: "To constitute suicide, the person must be of years of discretion and of a sound mind." Suicide happens when one ends his/her own life, with or without the aid of another person.

We have so many beliefs that are accepted as truth but have no scriptural foundation. We accept things as truth just because they have been said for a long time and loudly. It does not seem to matter that Scripture says otherwise.

Romans 3:3, 4 establishes a basic biblical principle:

"For what if some did not believe? shall their unbelief make the faith of God without effect?

"God forbid: yea, let God be true, but every man a liar; as it is written, That thou mightest be justified in thy sayings, and mightest overcome when thou art judged."

When what we think is different from what the Bible teaches, then what we think is wrong. Are we willing to set aside what we think, no matter how much we want to believe it, and accept what the Bible teaches? Remember, God alone is without error. What we think must always give way to Bible truth.

I want to share with you several examples of Bible characters who were brought to the point of wanting to die. We will look not only at their desire to die but also at what brought them to this point in their lives. Then I will share with you the help and hope the Bible gives those who are at such a point.

I also want to give some help to those who are suffering the terrible consequences of suicide.

Chapter 2

SIX THINGS THAT DROVE BIBLE CHARACTERS TO SEEK DEATH

There are several Bible stories of people who were brought to a point where they wanted to die. Some went to the Lord, seeking death at His hand; some killed themselves; and some just wanted to die.

Different emotions brought these people to despair. These same emotions can bring people to the point of suicide.

Within these stories, we find some of the same circumstances that tempt some present-day people to commit suicide. What drove these Bible characters to seek death?

Pain and Torment

"At that time, saith the LORD, they shall bring out the bones of the kings of Judah, and the bones of his princes, and the bones of the priests, and the bones of the prophets, and the bones of the inhabitants of Jerusalem, out of their graves:

"And they shall spread them before the sun, and the moon, and all the host of heaven, whom they have loved, and whom they have served, and after whom they have walked, and whom they have sought, and

*whom they have worshipped: they shall not be gath-
ered, nor be buried; they shall be for dung upon the face
of the earth.*

*"And death shall be chosen rather than life by all the
residue of them that remain of this evil family, which
remain in all the places whither I have driven them,
saith the LORD of hosts."*—Jer. 8:1–3.

The first kind of pain we see is emotional pain.
The children of Israel were about to experience
the judgment of God. They had spent years wor-
shiping the false gods of the heathen and ignoring
the warnings of God delivered by the prophets.
Now they were about to be defeated by the
Babylonian army. This army would come in and
take their freedom, their homes, and all things
dear to them.

The Babylonians would dig up the bones of the
kings and prophets of Israel and scatter those
bones on the ground under the sun. These were
the graves of those people that the Jews looked up
to and sought to imitate.

The Babylonians were going to take away the
Jews' identity. They were about to lose everything,
including their desire to live. This pain would be
more emotional than physical, but it would still
be pain.

We are wrong if we believe mental anguish to
be of no consequence. Many times mental anguish
can be more devastating than physical pain. One's

mental and emotional state often determines how he faces things physically. Sometimes it is easier to deal with a person in physical pain than a physically healthy person who is hurting emotionally. Emotional pain has many accomplices, thus making it a pain that must be dealt with.

There is a another kind of pain and torment:

"And the fifth angel sounded, and I saw a star fall from heaven unto the earth: and to him was given the key of the bottomless pit.

"And he opened the bottomless pit; and there arose a smoke out of the pit, as the smoke of a great furnace; and the sun and the air were darkened by reason of the smoke of the pit.

"And there came out of the smoke locusts upon the earth: and unto them was given power, as the scorpions of the earth have power.

"And it was commanded them that they should not hurt the grass of the earth, neither any green thing, neither any tree; but only those men which have not the seal of God in their foreheads.

"And to them it was given that they should not kill them, but that they should be tormented five months: and their torment was as the torment of a scorpion, when he striketh a man.

"And in those days shall men seek death, and shall not find it; and shall desire to die, and death shall flee from them."—Rev. 9:1–6.

This is an example of physical pain. The Bible teaches that before the Lord returns to earth to set up His kingdom, the earth will go through seven terrible years of judgment—the Tribulation.

During this time, the Lord will send terrible judgment upon man for all the wickedness of which man is guilty. One of the judgments will be the release of the creatures of Hell. These creatures will torment those who have the mark of the Beast.

The physical pain from these torments will be so intense that those afflicted by it will seek death but will not be able to die. The pain will be so great that it will drive many to attempt suicide in order to find relief from the pain, but all their attempts will be in vain, for the Lord will not allow them to die.

There are many who have reached the point where their physical pain is so intense that they would rather die than continue to live in pain.

I remember when my mother had gone through chemotherapy in her battle against cancer. When it looked like the cancer was returning, she said she would rather die than face another round of that awful treatment. The physical and emotional torment was more than she desired to bear.

For those of us who face periods of physical discomfort, it is hard to imagine what it would be like to face a lifetime of pain, knowing there is no relief from that pain this side of the grave.

To the Christian, suicide can be a tempting

option, especially when faced with the thought of a lifetime of pain. A lifetime of pain does not look appealing when compared to an eternity in Heaven.

"For I am in a strait betwixt two, having a desire to depart, and to be with Christ; which is far better:

"Nevertheless to abide in the flesh is more needful for you."—Phil. 1:23,24.

Heaven is at all times better than the best days on earth; much more so, the worst days. The best thing to happen to a Christian is to die and go to Heaven, especially when the days on earth are filled with pain and torment. To continue in a life of pain when an eternity in bliss awaits is not an easy assignment. To go to Heaven would be far better.

Many times the Lord uses the pain of an individual to prepare both the individual and his loved ones for death. Often a family is not ready to let their family member die. They hold onto every hope, every prayer, in an attempt to keep their loved one alive as long as possible. But when the pain becomes so intense, they start praying for the Lord to take their loved one.

My grandmother is an example of such a situation. She died when my mother was around eighteen years of age. Before she died, she was in so much pain that the family prayed for the Lord to take her. When the Lord finally took her, there

was a sense of both loss and relief. The Lord used
the pain to help the family deal with her death.

This is not to say that we should promote
doctor-assisted suicide, for the Lord must still be
the One to choose when it is time for a person to
die. Many times we can see no reason for prolong-
ing the agony, but we are not the Lord. We do not
have His perspective on things, nor do we see His
purpose and reasoning for a life to continue. We
must still give Him the right to work out His will
to completion.

Some people tire of hurting. Death seems to be
the only way out. If it is, then let the Lord determine the time, place and method. No doctor, psychiatrist, friend or family member has the right to
play God.

Escape From What Is Thought to Be a Worse Fate

Sometimes people see suicide as the only means
to avoid what they consider to be a worse fate.

*"And at midnight Paul and Silas prayed, and sang
praises unto God: and the prisoners heard them.*

*"And suddenly there was a great earthquake, so that
the foundations of the prison were shaken: and immediately all the doors were opened, and every one's bands
were loosed.*

*"And the keeper of the prison awaking out of his
sleep, and seeing the prison doors open, he drew out his*

sword, and would have killed himself, supposing that the prisoners had been fled."—Acts 16:25–27.

In this passage is the story of the Apostle Paul and Silas in jail at Philippi. At midnight the Lord sent an earthquake that caused both the doors of the prison and the stocks around their ankles to spring open.

Being awakened by the commotion, the jailer saw the doors open and assumed the prisoners had escaped. Rather than face the retribution of his superior officers, he chose to kill himself. He thought he knew his fate and decided that it would be better to die at his own hand than at the hands of his superiors. Had it not been for the Apostle Paul, the jailer probably would have succeeded in killing himself.

Another example of this thinking is seen in I Samuel 31:1–6:

"Now the Philistines fought against Israel: and the men of Israel fled from before the Philistines, and fell down slain in mount Gilboa.

"And the Philistines followed hard upon Saul and upon his sons; and the Philistines slew Jonathan, and Abinadab, and Melchi-shua, Saul's sons.

"And the battle went sore against Saul, and the archers hit him; and he was sore wounded of the archers.

"Then said Saul unto his armourbearer, Draw thy sword, and thrust me through therewith; lest these

uncircumcised come and thrust me through, and abuse me. But his armourbearer would not; for he was sore afraid. Therefore Saul took a sword, and fell upon it.

"And when his armourbearer saw that Saul was dead, he fell likewise upon his sword, and died with him.

"So Saul died, and his three sons, and his armourbearer, and all his men, that same day together."

We have read the story of the death of King Saul. Saul had been warned by the spirit of the Prophet Samuel that death was awaiting him in battle:

"Then said Samuel, Wherefore then dost thou ask of me, seeing the LORD is departed from thee, and is become thine enemy?

"And the LORD hath done to him, as he spake by me: for the LORD hath rent the kingdom out of thine hand, and given it to thy neighbour, even to David:

"Because thou obeyedst not the voice of the LORD, nor executedst his fierce wrath upon Amalek, therefore hath the LORD done this thing unto thee this day.

"Moreover the LORD will also deliver Israel with thee into the hand of the Philistines: and to morrow shalt thou and thy sons be with me: the LORD also shall deliver the host of Israel into the hand of the Philistines."—I Sam. 28:16–19.

We see the fulfillment of this prophecy in chapter 31. Saul had been shot by one of the Philistine archers. His wound was mortal. Death could not be avoided. He determined that to die quickly at his own hands was preferable to dying at the hands of the Philistines. He tried to get another to kill him but in the end did the deed himself.

He killed himself to avoid what he thought was a worse fate.

I am reminded of the story of the fewer than one thousand Jews who withstood an army of fifteen thousand Roman soldiers for nearly two years. They did so at a place called Masada, a fortress near the coast of the Dead Sea. The fortress was an area of about 18 acres, 1,424 feet above the Dead Sea, on the top of a mountain. When the soldiers finally reached the fortress, all but seven of the nearly one thousand Jews killed themselves rather than surrender to the Roman soldiers.

They chose suicide over what they saw as a worse fate.

Who of us has not heard stories of soldiers who, when wounded, killed themselves rather than be taken as prisoners? How many times have we heard of the wounded staying behind to face certain death so fellow soldiers could escape?

There are times when death seems to be a better fate than what lies ahead. Some people who face a life of paralysis or pain choose to die rather than experience such a life.

This frame of mind is reached more often than we may think. This is the thinking of those who support doctor-assisted suicide: death is rather to be chosen than a life of pain or debilitating disease.

I do not agree that this is an acceptable reason to commit suicide. I am just showing you some things that bring people to the point of suicide. (We will deal with this type of thinking later in the book.)

Sorrow of Heart

None in the Bible had to face a greater sorrow than Job. In one day he lost his livelihood, his livestock and his ten children. Job was a man dedicated to his family. He spent his life for the well-being of his children. Then the day came when the messengers brought him terrible news: "Job, you have lost it all." Job had done all he could to protect his children and raise them right.

"And it was so, when the days of their feasting were gone about, that Job sent and sanctified them, and rose up early in the morning, and offered burnt-offerings according to the number of them all: for Job said, It may be that my sons have sinned, and cursed God in their hearts. Thus did Job continually."—Job 1:5.

It would be great if fathers of our day were as concerned about the spiritual condition of their families as Job was about his family. There would be fewer delinquents if fathers took the spiritual condition of their children as a personal responsibility. Even with all Job's care, death still came to them. It seemed it was not supposed to end this way. He had not done anything that warranted such treatment. Look at Job's grief:

"Oh that I might have my request; and that God would grant me the thing that I long for!

"Even that it would please God to destroy me; that he would let loose his hand, and cut me off!

"Then should I yet have comfort; yea, I would harden myself in sorrow: let him not spare; for I have not concealed the words of the Holy One.

"What is my strength, that I should hope? and what is mine end, that I should prolong my life?"—Job 6:8–11.

In one day Satan took the lives of all ten of Job's children, leaving him a broken man. Satan was attacking Job in an effort to prove that Job served God only because God was good to him. It was actually Job's goodness that caused Satan to choose him. To suffer for wrong is one thing; to suffer for right is quite another, especially when God can prevent it.

But Job sat in the ashes, devastated from his loss. Look at Job's grief:

"But Job answered and said,

"Oh that my grief were throughly weighed, and my calamity laid in the balances together!

"For now it would be heavier than the sand of the sea: therefore my words are swallowed up."—Job 6:1–3.

The weight of his sorrow can only be imagined.

Just imagine the empty chairs around the table, the empty rooms and houses. The silence was a reminder of the death of his most cherished possessions. The weight was greater than that of the sand of the sea. The sorrow was of such great depth that words could not even come close to describing it.

What made it even worse was the fact that Job had no place to go for comfort. "For the arrows of the Almighty are within me, the poison whereof drinketh up my spirit: the terrors of God do set themselves in array against me" (Job 6:4). He did not have the Lord to go to, for the arrows in Job's heart were from the Lord. It would be very difficult to pray if one knew that the Lord was the cause for his broken heart.

He could not fight the Lord, nor could he change his situation. The only comfort he could see, humanly speaking, was in death.

Not only did Job lose his children, but his wife suffered the same loss. She could offer him no comfort, for she too was in need of comfort. No wonder she told Job to curse God and die; she was probably wanting to die. No comfort from God, no comfort from his wife, no comfort from friends—as a matter of fact, all his friends offered him was condemnation. What else was there to do but die?

Sometimes heartbreak is so great that it seems there is nothing to live for. This is usually when someone near and dear leaves by death or divorce, or when the children grow up and leave home, or when everything is lost in a disaster. When one experiences such sorrow of heart, it seems no one understands. It seems hard to find comfort in prayer, for even God does not seem to care. Those so afflicted think God just picked them out of the crowd and destined them to have their hearts crushed. No matter what they do, nothing seems to make their situation any better, and nothing is going to, because they have sorrow in the very essence of their souls.

Pressure

Some have desired death over life due to pressure. A great example of this is found in the story of Moses:

"And the mixt multitude that was among them fell a lusting: and the children of Israel also wept again, and said, Who shall give us flesh to eat?

"We remember the fish, which we did eat in Egypt freely; the cucumbers, and the melons, and the leeks, and the onions, and the garlick:

"But now our soul is dried away: there is nothing at all, beside this manna, before our eyes....

"Then Moses heard the people weep throughout their families, every man in the door of his tent: and the anger of the LORD was kindled greatly; Moses also was displeased.

"And Moses said unto the LORD, Wherefore hast thou

*afflicted thy servant? and wherefore have I not found
favour in thy sight, that thou layest the burden of all
this people upon me?*

*"Have I conceived all this people? have I begotten
them, that thou shouldest say unto me, Carry them in
thy bosom, as a nursing father beareth the sucking
child, unto the land which thou swarest unto their
fathers?*

*"Whence should I have flesh to give unto all this peo-
ple? for they weep unto me, saying, Give us flesh, that
we may eat.*

*"I am not able to bear all this people alone, because
it is too heavy for me.*

*"And if thou deal thus with me, kill me, I pray thee,
out of hand, if I have found favour in thy sight; and let
me not see my wretchedness."*—Num. 11:4–6, 10–15.

Moses was in a position that most people would
not be able to handle. The truth is, he could not
handle it either. He was the leader of an estimated
three million complaining Jews. He led them from
one impossible situation to another, and each time
they complained to him the more.

Can you imagine what it must have been like to
hear one complaint after another, continually?
"Moses, we're hungry. Moses, we're thirsty. Moses,
we want to go back to Egypt. Moses, we do not like
it here"—over and over, day in and day out, the
same complaints with no relief. When Moses
finally could stand it no longer, he came to the
Lord with one request, "Kill me."

Our society is just as unreasonable in its expectations. Teenage girls are under pressure to be Miss Perfect. Perfect looks, perfect eyes, perfect figure and perfect behavior are required by parents, teachers and friends.

Teenage boys are pressured to fit into the world's mold. They must possess and perform as the world says.

It is no different for parents: pressure at work from the boss, pressure at home from the family, pressure at church from the people—not to mention pressure from self.

Pressure from without, pressure from within, pressure from others and pressure from self are all self-imposed and self-destructive. Even the television adds to the pressure by giving some false sense of what life is supposed to be. After awhile, many turn to the bottle, drugs and even suicide.

Failed Expectations

Another area that has brought many to the point of desiring death is failed expectations. A great Bible example of this is the Prophet Elijah.

"And Ahab told Jezebel all that Elijah had done, and withal how he had slain all the prophets with the sword.

"Then Jezebel sent a messenger unto Elijah, saying, So let the gods do to me, and more also, if I make not thy life as the life of one of them by to morrow about this time.

"And when he saw that, he arose, and went for his life, and came to Beer-sheba, which belongeth to Judah, and left his servant there.

"But he himself went a day's journey into the wilderness, and came and sat down under a juniper tree: and he requested for himself that he might die; and said, It is enough; now, O LORD, take away my life; for I am not better than my fathers."—I Kings 19:1–4.

Running from Queen Jezebel, Elijah goes as far as his strength can take him, then sits under a juniper tree looking to God with a desire to die.

Humanly speaking, maybe he had a right to be discouraged. He had sacrificed for three and a half years after declaring the judgment of God.

At first he spent time at the brook Cherith and then with the widow at Zarephath. All that time he was fed either by the ravens or from a vessel of meal and oil, kept full by a miracle of God.

Elijah had stood against the four hundred fifty prophets of Baal and had beaten them. He stood against the king and prayed down fire from Heaven. He had gone up onto the mountain and prayed down rain, then had run to Jezreel to await the results. Surely he had the right to expect things to change. Surely the wicked King Ahab and Queen Jezebel would turn to the Lord.

Yet after all this, nothing had changed. They were still just as wicked. The people had not turned to the Lord, nor were they likely to.

Discouraged, disappointed and dejected, Elijah saw nothing left to do but to die.

Many have things all worked out in their minds. They live, sacrifice, plan, plot and give their whole lives for a dream, desire or goal, only to have it fall flat.

A great example is the 1929 stock market crash. Multiplied thousands were devastated by the loss of all their possessions and plans. Many saw nothing left to do but to commit suicide. They jumped to their deaths simply because their fortunes were wiped out.

Many a person has lost everything. The devastation coupled with the disappointment were so great they thought their only way out was by way of suicide.

Most people spend a lifetime looking forward to and planning for their retirement years. Just before that time, some tragedy comes, changing everything.

Some lose their mates just as they are beginning to live. Their big dreams go belly-up and become nightmares. Their hopes, their dreams and their expectations are dashed to the ground, leaving, as they think, nothing for which to live. When this point is reached, many choose suicide.

Failed expectations often lead to despair.

Another example of failed expectations is that of Jonah, another prophet sent by God.

"But it displeased Jonah exceedingly, and he was very angry.

"And he prayed unto the LORD, and said, I pray thee, O LORD, was not this my saying, when I was yet in my country? Therefore I fled before unto Tarshish: for I knew that thou art a gracious God, and merciful, slow to anger, and of great kindness, and repentest thee of the evil.

"Therefore now, O LORD, take, I beseech thee, my life from me; for it is better for me to die than to live.

"Then said the LORD, Doest thou well to be angry?

"So Jonah went out of the city, and sat on the east side of the city, and there made him a booth, and sat under it in the shadow, till he might see what would become of the city.

"And the LORD God prepared a gourd, and made it to come up over Jonah, that it might be a shadow over his head, to deliver him from his grief. So Jonah was exceeding glad of the gourd.

"But God prepared a worm when the morning rose the next day, and it smote the gourd that it withered.

"And it came to pass, when the sun did arise, that God prepared a vehement east wind; and the sun beat upon the head of Jonah, that he fainted, and wished in himself to die, and said, It is better for me to die than to live."—Jonah 4:1–8.

The expectations of Jonah were just the opposite of those of Elijah. Elijah sacrificed, desired to see revival, but did not. Jonah ran from God's call, did not want to see revival, but revival came anyway. In both cases they wanted to die as a result of their failed expectations.

Elijah wanted the Jews to repent, while Jonah wanted the people in Nineveh not to repent. He wanted them to pay for their crimes against the Jews.

The people of Nineveh were a wicked people and were about to face the judgment of God. The Lord sent Jonah to give them a chance at repentance, yet Jonah was not willing to go. He ran from the Lord, and the Lord sent a storm to bring him back.

The Lord sent a whale, but even then it took Jonah three days and nights in the whale's belly before he would pray. Then he was again sent to the wicked city.

Now he comes to a people guilty of things worse than he had ever done. Surely the people of Nineveh should be punished. But they repented, and judgment did not have to come.

Because of his bitter attitude, Jonah was brought to the point of anger at God and the world. It is out of this anger that he cries out to the Lord for death.

We are living in a time not much different from the times of Nineveh. People are living in disobedience and sin, not caring for the Lord or for His Word. The Christian, on the other hand, is trying to live for the Lord in this anti-God environment.

It is easy to get in the same mood as Jonah. It

is easy to see the wickedness of others and ignore our own rebellion. It is easy to get the attitude that "others are worse than I am; therefore, God will judge them before He judges me."

Proverbs 13:15 warns us, "The way of transgressors is hard." Life apart from the Lord is not supposed to work. People, whether saved or not, know they are not living a life pleasing to the Lord; but they continually live in sin, expecting all to turn out well. When it does not, they get bitter toward the Lord and have pity parties.

Many Christians assume that since others are more wicked then they, their own sin will go unnoticed by God. They see the wicked possessing the good things of life and think they themselves should be blessed with the same. When their situation is anything short of that, they say God is unfair.

Many times they get bitter and turn against the Lord. Like Jonah, seeking shade from the gourd to give him relief from the hot sun, they seek the comfort of their surroundings to relieve themselves of the discomfort of their situation. If the Lord removes this from them, they lie on the floor in self-pity and cry out about life being unfair.

The problem with them is as it was with both Elijah and Jonah. It is a problem fueled by self-centeredness and discontent. It comes when one has his eyes on himself and not on the Lord.

With this disappointment sometimes comes the thinking that leads to suicide.

Guilt

The greatest example of how far guilt can take someone is seen in Judas.

"When the morning was come, all the chief priests and elders of the people took counsel against Jesus to put him to death:

"And when they had bound him, they led him away, and delivered him to Pontius Pilate the governor.

"Then Judas, which had betrayed him, when he saw that he was condemned, repented himself, and brought again the thirty pieces of silver to the chief priests and elders,

"Saying, I have sinned in that I have betrayed the innocent blood. And they said, What is that to us? see thou to that.

"And he cast down the pieces of silver in the temple, and departed, and went and hanged himself."— Matt. 27:1–5.

You know the story of Judas and how he betrayed Jesus. The name *Judas* has become synonymous with deceit and betrayal. For thirty pieces of silver he became the chief of history's all-time bad guys. He betrayed the sinless Lamb of God with a kiss of friendship.

I personally believe he did not expect the people to put Jesus to death. I do know the Bible teaches that Satan entered him and led him in his betrayal.

"Then entered Satan into Judas surnamed Iscariot, being of the number of the twelve.

"And he went his way, and communed with the chief priests and captains, how he might betray him unto them.

"And they were glad, and covenanted to give him money.

"And he promised, and sought opportunity to betray him unto them in the absence of the multitude."— Luke 22:3–6.

After he betrayed the Lord, Judas returned to the priests the money of the betrayal, seeking to undo what he had done. The priests, however, didn't care about what Judas wanted: they finally had Jesus and were already in the process of putting Him to death.

When the priests refused to accept the money, Judas left in despair, went out and hung himself. He was driven by the guilt of his sin.

Sin always produces death, even when it seems like a person gets by with it. "Then when lust hath conceived, it bringeth forth sin: and sin, when it is finished, bringeth forth death" (Jas. 1:15). History is filled with the names of those who have died as a result of sin. One method of death is suicide.

I know of a man who at one time was a Sunday school teacher. He worked with teenagers and was a very active member of his church. He was employed for many years as a deputy with the sheriff's department.

After several years of faithful service, it was discovered that he had been molesting his granddaughter for a number of years. When the news started to get out, he decided that he would rather die than go to jail. With his service revolver he killed himself.

The guilt and consequences of sin always lead to death.

I know of a preacher who had been living in terrible sin for several years. Even though the people in his church knew about the situation, he continued to be the pastor of the church. No one, including preachers, can live in sin and get away with it. He started suffering from depression and eventually shot himself. Sin once again brought about death.

We have looked at six situations which brought Bible characters to the point where they wanted to die: pain and torment, escape from what is thought to be a worse fate, sorrow, pressure, failed expectations and guilt.

Circumstances can be devastating and bring about many terrible conclusions, but circumstances alone do not bring people to the point of suicide. Choosing suicide goes much deeper than the influence of circumstances.

In each Bible story, the main character came to

the point where he wanted to die, but only two of the characters considered committed suicide. The circumstances they were in were not unique to these men. "There hath no temptation taken you but such as is common to man: but God is faithful, who will not suffer you to be tempted above that ye are able; but will with the temptation also make a way to escape, that ye may be able to bear it" (I Cor. 10:13). The Bible promises that with every temptation comes a way to escape.

There is always a way for a person to make it through his situation. He is not destined to end his life with suicide, no matter what the situation. Suicide is a choice that is made, not an unavoidable destiny.

What is it about a situation that brings people to the point where they decide life is over? What brings some people to suicide and others to greater accomplishments?

Chapter 3

FOUR ATTITUDES OF DEPRESSED PEOPLE

In our society, people are not held responsible for their own actions. They have been programmed to look for a reason in something or someone else. Rather than accept responsibility for themselves, they blame society, parents, environment and circumstances.

A great example is that of a teenage boy who killed his girlfriend after she told him she was expecting a baby. His defense was that he should not be held responsible because his father abused him when he was a boy.

As the blame is shifted, so is the means of dealing with the problem. We seem more bent on trying to find an excuse than on trying to find the real cause and deal with it. We should not excuse our action but find the cause of the problem so we can find a solution.

There is a battle that is fought first in the mind, then completed with an act—the act of suicide.

We would do well if we could know the thoughts of any person who is contemplating suicide. I am not talking about psychology but human nature. We do not need to be psychiatrists to see the problem, nor do we need a doctor's degree to find the answer. All we need to do is to look at human nature. We do what we do because of what we are. The explanation is in the Word of God.

Do not let society deceive you into thinking you, together with the Lord, are not capable of solving your own problems. The psychiatric community has succeeded in convincing people today that the solutions to their problems are to be found on the psychiatrist's couch. They want us to believe that we are not capable of understanding the complexities of our situation, nor are we smart enough to figure out just how to solve our problems.

The solution is attainable, but the solution will not be found in the psychiatrist's office nor in the textbooks, but on the church pew and in your Bible.

As I looked at the Bible stories considered in the previous chapter, I found four emotions that were produced by the circumstances. Each emotion helped produce a desire to die. These emotions do not seem so dramatic when considered individually, but left unchecked, they mount up and, coupled with an improper view of God, can become deadly. Let's consider what the Bible has to say about each.

Helplessness

The first emotion that is evident is the sense of total helplessness.

King Saul in his chariot, wounded from the

archer's arrow, turns and sees the Philistine army in close pursuit. He realizes his life is almost over.

Notice the request he makes of his armor-bearer and the purpose of such a request: "Draw thy sword, and thrust me through therewith; lest these uncircumcised come and thrust me through, and abuse me" (I Sam. 31:4).

There was no way to change what was happening. King Saul was going to die. The only thing left to be decided was at whose hands he was going to die. He was in a situation in which there was no help. No doctors, no soldiers and no prophets would be coming to his rescue.

Moses, the great man of God, was burdened with all the cares of the people. He approaches the Lord with his request: "I am not able to bear all this people alone, because it is too heavy for me" (Num. 11:14).

Moses was at the end of his endurance. The people were complainers, the situation was one of hardship, the pressure was endless, and he saw no help in sight. He knew that his lot in life, at the age of eighty, was one of extreme difficulty.

We could look at the Philippian jailer, the Prophet Elijah, Moses, Saul, Jonah and many others. It is easy for us to say to them, "Just hang on," because we can read the rest of the story. However, they were not reading a story: they were living a life. Hindsight is a great source of comfort, but there is no hindsight when you are in the midst of a situation. All they knew was that they were in situations over which they had no control.

People basically want control—"my way, my plans, my effort." The Bible tells us in Isaiah 53:6: "All we like sheep have gone astray; we have turned every one to his own way." Often the biggest problem in certain situations is that people want control of their own lives. They basically want their own way. They do not like being told what to do, nor do they like being made to do anything. If they cannot be in control, they want out.

When considering suicide, people find themselves in situations they can no longer control. It is as if life has gotten out of control and has headed down a path to doom with no way of making any changes or of turning it around. They despair, because there is not one thing that can be done to change the outlook. The situations, as well as their solutions, are totally beyond their ability to control. The chain of events has been forged, and they cannot break it nor change it.

They feel like riders on a roller coaster with no way to get off. Once begun, the ride must be completed. At the end of the ride are despair, hopelessness and devastation. The only action left in their control is to jump off mid-ride—suicide.

If you have ever dealt with a suicidal person, you have seen this firsthand. Even people who are not suicidal want control. Most any person wants something he can do to change the situation he is in. Most anyone wants to be in charge.

Hopelessness

The emotion of hopelessness is similar to the emotion of helplessness and many times follows so closely to it, they both seem to be the same emotion. But as we study these two emotions in relation to suicide, we find they are two separate emotions. One can be in a helpless situation but still have hope that things will get better.

Hopelessness comes when a person sees no hope for change, when he finds himself in a situation he cannot control. He has no expectations of its getting better, nor can he see anything in the future in which to hope.

A great example of hopelessness is found in Job. He lost all he had in one day, and there was nothing he could do about it. His children were dead, his possessions stolen, his life turned upside down, and his heart broken. He saw the prospects of his future: "What is my strength, that I should hope? and what is mine end, that I should prolong my life?" (Job 6:11).

This verse is one of utter hopelessness. He was helpless to do anything about the situation, and he had no hope of its ever changing.

When some people go a period of time seeing no

help, they soon lose any sense of hope. Their focus is on changing the situation rather than coping with it. They believe the only way to make things better is to change the way things are. When people see an end in sight, they at least know the end is there, and that knowledge gives them some hope. If they cannot see the end, they often see no hope, no solution, and soon, no reason to live.

Some people facing a terminal illness reach this point. They believe death will come. They believe there is no hope for change, so they choose to end their own lives.

I am again reminded of the inmate in the Wilmington, North Carolina jail. He received a life sentence in one case, and it looked like two more life sentences were about to be handed down. Seeing no way to help resolve the situation and no hope of its getting any better, he ended his life.

Jonah ran from the Lord because he didn't like the job the Lord had for him to do. He fled to the port city of Tarshish, then booked passage on a ship headed for Joppa—all in an attempt to put distance between him and God.

But the Lord was not going to be deterred. He sent a storm into Jonah's path to thwart the plans of this wayward prophet.

All Jonah needed to do was submit to the Lord; instead, he chose to continue running from the Lord.

As the storm worsened, the sailors sought for

deliverance from their gods. Jonah, however, was asleep in the bottom of the ship. The sailors woke him and brought him face-to-face with his dilemma. They told him to pray to his God for their deliverance—probably the last thing he wanted to do.

Then they cast lots to see if the lots would reveal who was to blame for this dilemma. The Lord allowed the lot to fall upon Jonah.

With his sin revealed, he had no place to run. He saw he could not get away from the Lord; he was found out by man. He was in a helpless situation, with nowhere to run. He was helpless, then hopeless.

It was then that he requested to be thrown overboard. This backslidden prophet was willing to be cast into the sea, but he didn't want to do what God had called him to do. If it had not been for the Lord, Jonah would have died in the deep instead of being used to bring revival to a great city.

It is amazing how often this scenario is replayed. People run from the Lord because they want their own way. They don't like being told what to do, nor do they have a desire to do anything other than what *they* want to do.

The natural tendency of man is to go his own way. Even saved people rebel against God's call and plan. The Lord sends the storms of life to get their attention. They, however, do all in their power to get away from the Lord. When they see there is no escape, they lose all hope.

I have seen people in the midst of great tragedy who still would not turn to the Lord. People have intentions of getting right with God after they get through their trials. They do not seem to realize— nor are they willing to realize—that the Lord sent the hardships to get them to turn to Him rather than to solve the problems themselves.

Try as they may, they find no calming of the storm. Soon their helpless condition is accompanied by hopelessness. Soon they get to the end of themselves, and some take the next step, suicide.

Sorrow of Heart

Sorrow of heart settles in when a person loses all encouragement, drive or motivation. Another name for it is discouragement. Listen to the sorrow of heart spoken by Elijah the prophet: "It is enough; now, O LORD, take away my life; for I am not better than my fathers" (I Kings 19:4).

Elijah had done all that had been required of him. There were no more miracles that could be performed that would make any greater impact than the miracle he had already performed. The Lord had proven Himself to Elijah by caring for him for over three years. The Lord had proven Himself to the people by sending fire from

Heaven, then following it by rain, all at the request of Elijah.

When Elijah saw that Jezebel had not had a change of heart, he lost his drive and became discouraged, despondent and depressed. He lost his motivation, his encouragement and his expectation.

Another great example of sorrow of heart is found in Job. Look at the words of this discouraged, hurting, righteous man:

"Oh that my grief were throughly weighed, and my calamity laid in the balances together!

"For now it would be heavier than the sand of the sea: therefore my words are swallowed up."—Job 6:2,3.

Job personally knew sorrow. He experienced the feelings of helplessness and hopelessness, and then he had sorrow of heart. In the very center of his being he had sorrow. He was at the point where he could find nothing in which to be encouraged. The weight on his heart was more than he thought he could possibly bear. He saw no light at the end of the tunnel, no end to his valley.

When a person has sorrow of heart, his emotions are intensified. The problems take on a whole new dimension. All one can see is the impossibility.

One of the feelings a person has when faced with sorrow of heart is a feeling of being overwhelmed. All such a person can see is the magnitude of the problem. There is no amount of persuasion that can get one to see beyond the sorrow, for the sorrow has captivated all his attention. No amount of encouragement can overcome the feeling of devastation or inadequacy. The burden seems to weigh as much as the sand of the sea. It seems as vast as the ocean, as endless as space. The sorrowing person can see no way out of his situation, even if many escape routes are within view.

When one is sorrowing in this way, it is important to remember that the situation is not the problem, but the person's attitude is. Such an attitude carries consequences worse than the surrounding problems. (We will continue with this train of thought later in the chapter.)

There is another emotion experienced by those suffering sorrow of heart. Read more of what Elijah experienced with sorrow of heart: "And he said, I have been very jealous for the LORD God of hosts: for the children of Israel have forsaken thy covenant, thrown down thine altars, and slain thy prophets with the sword; and I, even I only, am left; and they seek my life, to take it away" (I Kings 19:10).

Elijah felt he was alone, no one was left to stand with him, he was the last line of defense, and the enemy was too big. His thoughts were so wrapped up in self-pity that he forgot about the widow and her son with whom he had stayed during the famine. He forgot about Obadiah and the prophets he had safely hidden from the evil king. There were many more people on God's side than Elijah realized.

When one has sorrow of heart, he sees himself as being all alone: no one else seems to have it as rough as he, nor does anyone else understand just how rough it really is. When one is in this condition, anyone who offers any way out just does not truly understand the totality nor the severity of the situation. "If they only knew how bad it really is, they would realize that there is no way out."

I have had to deal with people in such a frame of mind. Sometimes when they come asking for advice they only want a place to vent their sorrow and frustration. Any advice is met immediately with an excuse for why it will not work.

The reason for this is, when discouragement sets in, a person does not think clearly. If you have ever tried to deal with one in the midst of sorrow of heart, you know the frustration. No matter how much truth you give him, he does not seem any better. It seems that he refuses to accept any conclusion other than what he has already accepted as truth.

The word *discourage* means "to extinguish the courage of; to dishearten; to depress the spirits, to deprive of confidence." People lose all encouragement, joy and hope. They can see only the dark side of every situation. They are without any motivation or drive even to seek a solution, because they don't believe there is one. Some see only one thing as a "solution"—suicide—and anything other than that is no solution at all.

The book of Proverbs deals in some detail with the subject of sorrow of heart. By studying it, we can see why it is so hard to deal with a person with sorrow of heart. Proverbs reveals the characteristics of sorrow of the heart by first giving us the opposite end of the emotional spectrum, then revealing sorrow's equivalent.

As you look at these verses, keep in mind the suicidal person and see if you can see in him what is revealed in these proverbs:

"A merry heart maketh a cheerful countenance: but by sorrow of the heart the spirit is broken."—Prov. 15:13.

The merry heart is the opposite of the sorrowful heart. It is what we should and many times do experience. It is what the world is looking for and what those who are suicidal do not have.

When a person has a merry heart he will have a cheerful countenance. In the Hebrew, the word *cheerful* means "to be causative, make well, sound, beautiful, happy, successful." When a person has a merry heart, he has a happy, successful outlook. He sees the beauty of the situation and its possibilities, making life not only bearable but enjoyable.

Sorrow of heart is just the opposite. When a person is wounded in the very essence of his being, he loses all drive. The spirit is afflicted, taking away any positive outlook on anything. When a person has a broken spirit, he sees no possibilities, no beauty, nothing in which to be encouraged. He loses all drive because he sees no motive for living, no great expectations for the future. A person in this condition sees nothing in which to be encouraged, no matter what you show him.

"A merry heart doeth good like a medicine: but a broken spirit drieth the bones."—Prov. 17:22.

Now we see the merry heart is like a medicine. The words *doeth good* come from the same Hebrew word from which we get the word *maketh* in Proverbs 15:13.

Just as a merry heart affects one's outlook, it also affects his very nature. It is the healing force in any situation. When a person has a merry heart, he can find the solution to his situation, or at least a way to endure it. However, those who are of a broken spirit find nothing within themselves in which to be hopeful.

The word *drieth* means to be ashamed, confused and disappointed. There are no direction, no pride, no joy and definitely no inward peace. All one can see is the situation and the heartache it brings.

"All the days of the afflicted are evil: but he that is of a merry heart hath a continual feast."—Prov. 15:15.

This passage in Proverbs seems to put the

whole thing into perspective. Every day is a bad day to those with sorrow of heart. Every event, every situation, every circumstance and every possibility are only negative. To those who have a merry heart there is something good that can be found even in bad days.

To those with sorrow of heart there is no good in anything. No matter what you say to them, what hope you try to give them or how encouraging you are, they can always find the bad; and the bad will always outweigh the good. Once discouraged, they really don't want a solution nor an encouraging word. They have no desire to do anything constructive, for they can see no benefit in it.

This is why it is so frustrating to try to help a person in this mood. If he had a different frame of mind, the words of encouragement would build him up. But as he is, nothing one can say is of any help. It is the heart, not the situation, that is the problem.

This is an important point for any reader who is experiencing sorrow of heart. You have lost your drive, your motivation and your perspective, enabling you to see only the bad in everything. You need to realize that the situation is not the real problem: the real problem is that your spirit has been wounded.

Your emotional wound is as real as any bullet wound a person might have. The bullet wound has consequences; so does the emotional wound. The bullet wound bleeds, gets infected and must be doctored. Left untreated, it can lead to death.

The emotional wound also has its consequences. It affects the outlook and the emotions. It makes you see only the pain, not the possibilities. The important thing to remember is that what you are feeling right now is what is controlling your perception of things.

There are hope and help for the broken spirit. (We will look at some of the cures later in this book.)

Weariness of Life

Weariness of life was best expressed by Job:

"My soul is weary of my life; I will leave my complaint upon myself; I will speak in the bitterness of my soul."—Job 10:1.

Job finally reached the breaking point. He was tired of the helplessness, hopelessness and the sorrow of heart. He was to the point where he felt there was no need to continue on.

My mother expressed it in a similar way when she said, "I'm just tired of being sick all the time." There are times when a person just wants the pain, be it emotional or physical, to stop. He has reached the point where he is too weary to take another step.

Elijah had reached this point when he said, "It

is enough; now, O LORD, take away my life; for I am not better than my fathers" (I Kings 19:4).

Moses had reached the same point when he said,

"I am not able to bear all this people alone, because it is too heavy for me.

"And if thou deal thus with me, kill me, I pray thee, out of hand, if I have found favour in thy sight; and let me not see my wretchedness."—Num. 11:14,15.

Jonah expressed the same thing when he said, "It is better for me to die than to live" (Jonah 4:3).

With no strength, no help, no encouragement and no hope, each man had reached the point where he wanted to die.

It is hard to give encouragement to people who have reached such a point. They think they are the only ones who truly understand, for surely if others understood, they would see it exactly the same way. They feel encouragement offered is misunderstanding revealed. They know they cannot help themselves, for they have lost all hope of any change for the better. They have no motivation to continue and are tired of living in this condition. The only solution they can see is death.

Is there any help for people when they reach this point? The answer is yes.

Chapter 4

THE DECISION

Before we look at the hope the Bible gives to those contemplating suicide, it would be beneficial to present one more aspect of the Bible stories as we have read them. Of the people of whom we have read—the Israelites, the Philippian jailer, King Saul, Job, Moses, Elijah, Jonah and Judas—we find two outcomes. Two found no reason to continue, and they committed suicide. The others seemed to find something on which to rest, something that brought them through their diffficulties.

As I look at these stories, I find an important truth that must be considered if the rest of this book will be of any help. There is a reason why some people survive and others do not. The whole subject of suicide and its solution rests upon this point.

Those whom I have been able to help deal with their problems had to come to grips with the point of this chapter. The difference in the success or failure of dealing with those who are facing the difficulties of life is found in this great Bible truth. The thing that makes the difference is the decision that is made, but what is this decision?

As we think back on our stories, let's look again at what each of these Bible characters had to face.

The Israelites mentioned in the book of Jeremiah and those found in the book of Revelation were facing both emotional and physical pain. The jailer and King Saul were facing a fate they perceived worse than death. Job, the great example of the one who suffered such extreme sorrow, cursed the day in which he was born and desired the Lord to bring an end to his days. Moses was called upon to deal with pressures beyond his capabilities to handle. Two prophets suffered depression caused by failed expectations. We concluded the list by looking at Judas who had to deal with a guilt so strong that he allowed it to drive him to suicide.

Of these listed, two committed suicide. Of those mentioned in Revelation, many will try to commit suicide yet will not be able to die. What caused, or will cause, them to give up? What caused the others to keep going? What is the difference between those who give life another chance and those who finish it by one last desperate act?

The conclusions of two of the stories illustrate the point of this chapter:

"And the battle went sore against Saul, and the archers hit him; and he was sore wounded of the archers.

"Then said Saul unto his armourbearer, Draw thy sword, and thrust me through therewith; lest these uncircumcised come and thrust me through, and abuse me. But his armourbearer would not; for he was sore afraid. Therefore Saul took a sword, and fell upon it."— I Sam. 31:3,4.

I see two things in King Saul's predicament: First, he saw no way out of his situation. He saw in the immediate future a humiliating death at the hands of the Philistines. Second, he did what he deemed as his only option—he fell upon his own sword.

The next story is that of Elijah:

"And when he saw that, he arose, and went for his life, and came to Beer-sheba, which belongeth to Judah, and left his servant there.

"But he himself went a day's journey into the wilderness, and came and sat down under a juniper tree: and he requested for himself that he might die; and said, It is enough; now, O LORD, take away my life; for I am not better than my fathers."—I Kings 19:3, 4.

Here we find the Prophet Elijah discouraged, disappointed and depressed. His perception of his situation was in some ways like King Saul's view of his. He thought that the best he could do was not good enough to change his situation. After three and a half years of sacrifice, nothing had changed, nor was it about to. He came to the Lord with the only way he could see to resolve the situation: "Kill me."

The Lord, however, had a different solution to the problem: "And the Lord said unto him, Go, return on thy way to the wilderness of Damascus: and when thou comest, anoint Hazael to be king over Syria" (I Kings 19:15). The Lord's response was for him to "go, return." The Lord was not done with Elijah and showed him that even in the midst of depression, the work of God continues.

Notice Elijah's response after meeting with the Lord: "So he departed thence, and found Elisha the son of Shaphat, who was plowing with twelve yoke of oxen before him, and he with the twelfth: and Elijah passed by him, and cast his mantle upon him" (I Kings 19:19).

Elijah left the mountain cave and went to find Elisha. Elijah continued beyond the point where King Saul stopped.

In each of these stories you find the same scenario. Each of these Bible characters faced his own hopeless situation, and they all came to the same conclusion: the only way to resolve the problem was in death.

Judas thought only one thing would get him out of his predicament—he hung himself. He thought only one thing would stop the guilt—suicide. The jailer, on the other hand, stopped short of his intentions; he put away his sword and listened to Paul. The stories of these men go in opposite directions.

Moses followed the Lord's command rather than continuing in his self-pity. He allowed the Lord to pull him out of his despair and appointed seventy men to help deal with the pressure.

Job sat in the ashes that remained of his life and scraped the boils sent by the Devil. In the midst of his despair "Job sinned not, nor charged God foolishly" (Job 1:22). A great description of Job's response to his difficulties is found in Job 2:10: "In all this did not Job sin with his lips." Job turned the situation over to the Lord.

I believe the attitude of Job reflects that of each who trusted the Lord rather than turning to suicide.

"Then Job answered the LORD, and said,

"I know that thou canst do every thing, and that no thought can be withholden from thee."—Job 42:1,2.

Job trusted the Lord to be able to do everything necessary to be done. He also believed the Lord knew when things needed to be done. Job did not blame God for, nor charge Him with the fault for, his circumstances. He simply let the Lord deal with the situation at hand.

The difference between those who commit suicide and those who do not is in who is given control of the situation. Those who commit suicide have taken the reins of their lives in their own hands. They have taken charge of the situation and finding its solution. What they do not realize is that they are not capable of resolving the situation. The hopelessness of trusting self is demonstrated by the "solution" arrived at by the two who committed suicide.

They also came to their own conclusions. They not only came to a conclusion as to what the problem was but also as to what were the cause and result of and solution to the problem. They concluded that there was no other solution or way out other than the one at which they had arrived. They concluded how and when the situation was to stop—suicide. They took complete control away from the Lord.

The Christian, however, should know the futility of taking matters into his own hands. He should know that the Lord has been and always will be the One with the answers. The Lord is the One with the plan for living life with an abundance. He is also the One who controls the situations in which we find ourselves. "My times are in thy hand: deliver me from the hand of mine enemies, and from them that persecute me" (Ps. 31:15). Our times, good or bad, are in the hands of the Lord. Our situations in life are under His control.

When confronted with this point, many will start to complain about the way the Lord has handled their situations. They speak of the Lord as being unfair and partial, attributing to Him the weaknesses of man. They accuse the Lord of doing something wrong or unwise. They behave as if the Lord has made a gross error in judgment. They speak of their own rights and of how the Lord has greatly mistreated them.

The Bible's response to these complaints is not what most people in this frame of mind want to hear: The Lord is the sovereign God. He has the right, as well as the wisdom, to do whatever He chooses. He is our Creator, the Almighty God of the universe. He is the great "I Am." The Lord put it this way when first dealing with a delivered Israel:

"I am the LORD thy God, which have brought thee out of the land of Egypt, out of the house of bondage.

"Thou shalt have no other gods before me."—Exod. 20:2, 3.

He is the Lord, not you or I. To question God and to take control from Him is to rebel against His authority. That is an earmark of unsaved, unregenerate men: "All we like sheep have gone astray; we have turned every one to his own way; and the Lord hath laid on him the iniquity of us all" (Isa. 53:6). The natural response of mankind is to want his own way; but the Lord is the Supreme Ruler of all creation, for it all belongs to Him.

"For by him were all things created, that are in heaven, and that are in earth, visible and invisible, whether they be thrones, or dominions, or principalities, or powers: all things were created by him, and for him:

"And he is before all things, and by him all things consist.

"And he is the head of the body, the church: who is the beginning, the firstborn from the dead; that in all things he might have the preeminence."—Col. 1:16–18.

He is to have the preeminence in all things, for He is the preeminent One.

What does this have to do with suicide, and how did it play a part in our Bible stories? First, those who committed suicide were not willing to entrust their situation to the Lord. They had to control the situations, even if it meant death. Those who found life through and beyond their trying circumstances did so because they recognized the Lord as the one in charge. They simply left their situations in the Lord's hands. They realized that the Lord should be in charge, and He has the right to do with our lives whatever He chooses. If He sees that we need a period of hardship, then He has the right to bring about that hardship and expect us to follow Him through it.

Another thing to be considered when one has the idea of suicide is the value of the life he is contemplating ending. He may look at his life filled with its problems and see in it nothing of value. He may see nothing but heartache and headaches. He may see a life that has reached its lowest ebb with no way for it to get any better. He begins to see his life as not being worth very much. He sees the value of his life as not being worth the pain in which he finds himself.

Here is another great truth: each life has value. Each life has a price, a net worth, a bottom line. A person's life is not the worthless occupation of time which he might perceive it to be at any given moment. It is not wasted, nor would anything necessarily be improved if a life ended. Each person has a valuable gift. Life is worth more than all the possessions of all the people who have ever lived or will ever live. It has both a temporal and an eternal value. In what areas can this great value be found?

Each life has value because life itself is valuable. Even Satan knows the value that man puts on life. "And Satan answered the Lord, and said, Skin for skin, yea, all that a man hath will he give for his life" (Job 2:4). It is hard to know just how valuable is one more day on this earth. People spend their whole life savings just to prolong their time on this earth for only a few more days.

The value of life is not judged alone by its possession; it is also valued by the joy that life produces. Value depends upon that which is spent. Life is made up of time spent. The value of that time is determined by the value of the things on which it is spent. Life is a valuable thing, but not just because of its material possessions and conditions.

All life, no matter what its condition or duration, has value. It is a value that cannot be measured in tangible things, but it is value nevertheless. The value is that which the Lord placed upon it.

Why is a life valuable? First, it has value because it is life. "And the Lord God formed man of the dust of the ground, and breathed into his nostrils the breath of life; and man became a living soul" (Gen. 2:7). God made man different from anything else in His creation. He breathed His breath into us, and we became a living soul.

Christ came into the world to give us life. "I am come that they might have life, and that they might have it more abundantly" (John 10:10). We have a special place in the heart of God. The love God has for the world (John 3:16) is the same love He has for each one of us. We are His special creation.

This question has been asked for years: "If we are so special, then why are there so many problems?" The answer is quite simple: Because of Adam's sin in the Garden, life has been difficult. Man survives by the sweat of his brow. Life consists of days which are few and full of troubles. "Man that is born of a woman is of few days, and full of trouble" (Job 14:1). The life we live on this earth is not supposed to be Heaven. It is a life that is spent in the midst of sin and death. Life, especially that of the transgressor, is hard. Many times the life of the righteous is equally as hard; but a hard life is not a life of no value, nor is a life of ease necessarily a life of value.

Everyone will come to a point in his life when the day loses its pleasure. "Remember now thy Creator in the days of thy youth, while the evil days come not, nor the years draw nigh, when thou shalt say, I have no pleasure in them" (Eccles. 12:1). There will come a time when the pains of life will overshadow its joys.

If one esteems the value of his life to be in its

pleasures and ease, when he is in the circumstance described in Ecclesiastes 12:1, he will think his life no longer has value. Hard times are a part of life, and many times the sole purpose of them is to give added value to life. We must learn to see beyond the moment.

Life has value because of what it represents. "Whoso sheddeth man's blood, by man shall his blood be shed: for in the image of God made he man" (Gen. 9:6). The value of your life is not just in its possession; it is also in its purpose. Mankind was made in the image of God. When God made the earth, He did so for His glory. On this earth, He left us illustrations of His power, wisdom and character.

"Because that which may be known of God is manifest in them; for God hath shewed it unto them.

"For the invisible things of him from the creation of the world are clearly seen, being understood by the things that are made, even his eternal power and Godhead; so that they are without excuse."—Rom. 1:19,20.

The Lord has revealed Himself to man through His creation. The orderliness of God is seen in the order of nature. The holiness of God is seen in the perfection of His original creation and is contrasted against the corruption of man since his fall.

Another example of God's character and nature is in the creation of mankind. Man was created to picture the authority of God over the creation of

God. We see in the Scripture that man represents God and the creation of man testifies to the relationship God desires with us. The woman represents man, and her submission to her husband is to show the relationship man is to have with God. Even the way a person wears his hair and dresses depicts this relationship which God desires with man.

We are living illustrations of the truth the Lord wants people to know. We were given dominion over the world, for we represent the supremacy of God.

A person's life is not his own, especially if he is saved. His life has value because it is God's illustration. For one to take his own life is to pervert the image that God has placed here on earth.

"What? know ye not that your body is the temple of the Holy Ghost which is in you, which ye have of God, and ye are not your own?

"For ye are bought with a price: therefore glorify God in your body, and in your spirit, which are God's."—I Cor. 6:19, 20.

A believer's life also has value because of what God has given him. God has placed within each believer the Holy Spirit. Because of this relationship a man can have fellowship with God.

God placed within Adam the ability to communicate with God. When Adam sinned, this ability died within him. In Jesus we have new life. Our spirit is made alive. We now not only have access to God but also fellowship with Him. This makes our lives of great value. We can have access to the Creator of the universe, and He considers this relationship of great value; after all, He died to secure this life for us.

A Christian's life has value because of its potential. "Verily, verily, I say unto you, He that believeth on me, the works that I do shall he do also; and greater works than these shall he do; because I go unto my Father" (John 14:12). The Lord has placed the Holy Spirit within you not only to establish fellowship with you but also to provide you with the wherewithal to accomplish even greater things than Jesus did on this earth— greater things, because you have a longer ministry on earth than Jesus had when He was here. The worthwhileness of your life is enhanced because it is built upon all that has happened before and added to all that will happen in the future. We can do "greater works" because the Lord has determined to do greater things through us than He did Himself. Your potential is not in your abilities but in His ability to use you. To have a life of usefulness to the Lord is to have a life of great value.

The difference between those who committed suicide and those who did not is not in the circumstances of their lives, but in their outlook. Some saw the supremacy of God and yielded their lives, with all their problems, to Him. They left it all in the Lord's hands and simply continued in the direction He led. They trusted the Lord to work things out, and they were not disappointed.

On the other hand, those who took matters into their own hands quickly came to the end of their rope. After all their effort, they could find no better solution than to take their own lives.

The difference between those who committed suicide and those who did not is in the value they placed on their own lives. Some saw their lives as having value. They were valuable because they were God-given. They were valuable because of what they represented and that which they had been given, namely, the ability to know and fellowship with the Lord. Their lives had value, for they had potential.

The difference between the two groups lies in the fact that those who survived saw the Lord as the one in control. They did not question God, nor did they charge Him foolishly. They knew the Lord had the right to ask of them what He would, even a life of hardship. They did not rebel, for they belonged to the King.

Each person contemplating suicide must decide in whose hands he will place his life. The decision is in what he sees as the value of his life. Is the value of a life found only in its pleasures? Is the value of a life found in the things that really have no redeeming value? Is the value of a life found in its possession, its potential and its possibilities? Is the value of a life found in the things that God has declared valuable? The difference between life and death, between hope and despair, between suicide and abundant living is determined by who is allowed to have complete control.

Chapter 5

THE RESULTS OF SUICIDE

Before we look at the help we can offer those who are suffering from helplessness, hopelessness, sorrow of heart and weariness of life, we look at the aftermath of suicide. What are the results of suicide? Does suicide really solve the problem, or does it just make matters worse? What does the Bible have to say about this?

When a person commits suicide, he usually has an idea of how he thinks circumstances are going to turn out. He usually sees suicide as a means for making the problems go away. It is usually thought of as a way of making things better for himself. Sometimes a person thinks suicide will improve the situation for others involved. What a suicidal person does not realize is that there is an aftermath that accompanies suicide.

Sometimes a person chooses suicide as a means of punishing others. He has the idea that when those left behind realize that they were the cause of the suicide, they will spend the rest of their lives in sadness. He has the idea of using the sorrow as a punishment for them. I know of one young man who committed suicide because his girlfriend broke up with him. His intention was to teach her a lesson. His thought was that she would suffer like he had been suffering. What he did not realize was that his suffering was just beginning.

No matter what the reasoning behind it, suicide carries some extremely heavy consequences. It creates problems and situations that many times cannot ever be overcome. It can create problems that will last for generations. Suicide not only affects the one who commits it; it affects an unknown number of other people. The results of suicide do not end with the last breath; they will continue for eternity.

What are some of the results of suicide?

Suicide and Others

The first thing to consider is the ramifications that suicide has on others. The person contemplating suicide usually has his eyes on himself. He sees the problem as it affects him only. Many times he does not realize that one selfish action will have an effect that will be felt for all eternity.

Any one person's suicide will affect others. "For none of us liveth to himself, and no man dieth to himself" (Rom. 14:7). No person dies truly alone. When a person dies, all his opportunities die with him. When a person dies, his labors, his vision and much of his influence die with him. All the good that he could have done will be left undone, and all those who would have benefited from that good will have to do without it. Suicides may have the idea that someone else will pick up the slack, but that is not usually the case. When I have had to deal with those left behind, I have always found a terrible path of destruction left in the suicide's wake.

The aftermath of suicide, especially that of a Christian, includes a detrimental effect on the cause of Christ. As Christians we have a testimony to uphold before a lost and dying world. The world is looking to us, for we are the salt of the earth and the light of the world. When the world sees us, they see the ones who are supposed to have the answers to life's questions. They see those who are supposed to be able not only to find the right thing to do but also to do it. Some see us as the only Bible they will ever read. How we live and die determines whether they listen to what we have to say.

This past week I was told of a man from Czechoslovakia who put off salvation for many years because a Christian friend of his from the old country had committed suicide. He had trouble believing there was anything to this thing called "Christianity." No matter what anyone else said to him, the action of that one person was all Satan needed to provide him with an excuse for not being saved.

If you commit suicide, you will be providing Satan with another weapon to add to his arsenal. You will cause people to look at the story of salvation as nothing more than a sweet bedtime story for children. You will be robbing people of a blissful eternity. I have had to deal personally with unsaved ones who knew of a Christian who took his own life. Those people were hardhearted toward the Gospel. They could not see beyond the suicide, no matter what Scripture I presented. They looked at the Gospel as being weak and somewhat defective.

I was pastor of a church where a former pastor had committed suicide. I met several people who had attended the church at the time of the suicide. Most of them were out of church—the sad influence of suicide.

If you commit suicide, you will never have a chance to witness to some people. The Lord has called us all to be witnesses. He has promised to use us to bear fruit, if we will allow Him to do so. If you take your life, all those people to whom you would have given a gospel witness will die without your witness. You may have been the one to whom they would have listened; but if you choose to commit suicide, they will not have the benefit of your witness. They will lose another opportunity to be saved. All the labor you could have done will be left undone. All the blessing you could have been, will not be. All the benefits you could have provided to others will not be handed out.

There is a certain spot in life which only you can fill. If you commit suicide, your spot will be empty. There never has been, nor will there ever be, another you.

There will never be a second chance for those who end their lives. Life is lived only once.

The suicide of one will produce a reaction in others. A good example of this is seen in King Saul's armorbearer. "And when his armourbearer saw that Saul was dead, he fell likewise upon his sword, and died with him" (I Sam. 31:5). Because of Saul's action, his armorbearer also took his own life.

I dealt with the son of a man who committed suicide. He was a young adult who, like his father, was prone to depression. He seemed to be following the steps of his father. He will always have in the back of his mind the option of suicide. The suicide of one will bring to the minds of others the possibility of their own suicide. I have seen cases where one suicide led to others.

Another thing to consider is the testimony that will not be given. The world cannot argue with one who, with the Lord's help, withstood the odds and triumphed. When one commits suicide, he robs people of that stirring challenge. The greater the obstacles, the greater the power of the testimony. Our favorite stories are of those who against all odds stood alone. The greatest testimony is a personal one. The greatest examples of courage are those who refuse to give in or give up, those who trust the Lord no matter what. This type of testimony can come only from a life that is lived against the odds, the life of one who stands while others fall.

Suicide and the Unsaved

There is another aspect of suicide that many do not consider: Suicide does not stop the problems. The general idea of the suicide is that death will end the problems, that they will be over. The truth is, however, when one's body dies, his soul lives on. Whether lost or saved, a person's situations do not stop with death. Once death occurs, there will be no escaping the consequences of life and the decisions made during it.

Those who are not saved—those who have not trusted the Lord as their personal Saviour—will begin experiencing an eternal torment that will make all the headaches and heartaches of this life seem like child's play.

I am reminded of the inmate who killed himself in the New Hanover County Jail. He did so because he did not want to face imprisonment for the rest of his life. His thought was that he would be free; he would have no more jail, jailers and trials. He thought all those would end for him. What he did not realize was that he was about to enter an eternal imprisonment. He did not realize that he would stand before the one true, holy judge and would have no defense and no hope of acquittal.

"And I saw a great white throne, and him that sat on it, from whose face the earth and the heaven fled away; and there was found no place for them.

"And I saw the dead, small and great, stand before

God; and the books were opened: and another book was opened, which is the book of life: and the dead were judged out of those things which were written in the books, according to their works.

"And the sea gave up the dead which were in it; and death and hell delivered up the dead which were in them: and they were judged every man according to their works.

"And death and hell were cast into the lake of fire. This is the second death.

"And whosoever was not found written in the book of life was cast into the lake of fire."—Rev. 20:11–15.

What this fellow expected and what happened were two different things. He expected release, but he received bondage. He expected life to be better; but instead, he lifted his eyes in torment.

"And it came to pass, that the beggar died, and was carried by the angels into Abraham's bosom: the rich man also died, and was buried;

"And in hell he lift up his eyes, being in torments, and seeth Abraham afar off, and Lazarus in his bosom."—Luke 16:22,23.

The moment he entered eternity, he entered a hell that will never be stopped and where there is no suicide. He found out that his life of affliction and hardship suddenly became a million times worse. He found himself doomed to hell for all eternity.

"Then shall he say also unto them on the left hand,

Depart from me, ye cursed, into everlasting fire, prepared for the devil and his angels."—Matt. 25:41.

"And the smoke of their torment ascendeth up for ever and ever: and they have no rest day nor night, who worship the beast and his image, and whosoever receiveth the mark of his name."—Rev. 14:11.

If you are unsaved and think it cannot get any worse, please think again. The Bible teaches that you have already been tried and condemned. There will be no trial to determine if you should or should not go to Heaven, for the judgment has already been passed. The Lord has already ruled that all who die lost must go to eternal damnation in a place called Hell. "He that believeth on him is not condemned: but he that believeth not is condemned already, because he hath not believed in the name of the only begotten Son of God" (John 3:18). The moment you take your life, you will enter an eternal torment such as cannot be imagined.

One of the torments of Hell will be the never-ending thought that you are there because you placed yourself there; you are there because you did not accept the only provision God made to avoid Hell. "Jesus answered and said unto him, Verily, verily, I say unto thee, Except a man be born again, he cannot see the kingdom of God" (John 3:3). You not only will be there, but you will be there early because you took your own life. You will spend all eternity regretting the decision you made to commit suicide and especially the decision you made to reject salvation.

You will be in Hell, not because you committed suicide but because you died unsaved; you died without a Saviour; you died with not only the sins of your life on your record but also the sin of your death on your record. Suicide is a sin, and you will stand before God and give an account of it as well as all your other sins. You will have missed the forgiveness of God. You will stand before God on your own merits, and they are not good enough. "For all have sinned, and come short of the glory of God" (Rom. 3:23).

If you are unsaved, put your trust in the Lord today for your salvation. Let Him save your soul, then trust Him with your troubles. Please do not make the worst mistake you could ever make for all eternity—that of rejecting Christ. Once death has come, it will be too late to be saved.

The Bible teaches there will be two judgments: one judgment for the saved and the other judgment for the lost. Those who die without Christ, those who die unsaved, will be at the great white throne judgment, where the degree of their punishment in the lake of fire will be determined.

The judgment of Revelation 20:11–15 is for those who are dead. Who are the dead spoken of here? "And you hath he quickened, who were dead in trespasses and sins" (Eph. 2:1). The unsaved person is already dead, condemned to spend eternity in a Devil's Hell (John 3:18). The dead will be judged according to the things that have been recorded by God.

What is being recorded? According to Revelation 20:13, "their works." This means all the things a person has ever done, including suicide. This means that a lost person who kills himself not only must give an account to God for all his previous sins but must add to that list the sin of suicide. It will be another sin for which he will be punished. There will be another charge and another degree of punishment added to his sentence, and he will have to deal with the suicide throughout eternity. While the pain of the suicide may be eased to a degree in the hearts of the saddened loved ones on earth, it will be forever fresh on the mind of the lost person in Hell.

Suicide and the Christian

This is an area of controversy. I have met many who believe that if a person commits suicide, he has lost his salvation. "You cannot commit suicide and go to Heaven," they say. "He could not have been a Christian if he committed suicide!" On the contrary, people who call themselves Christian have committed or will yet commit suicide.

Is it possible for a professing Christian to kill himself and still go to Heaven? Many people call suicide "self-murder." Their belief is that one cannot go to Heaven if he has murdered someone, especially himself. Others believe one cannot go to Heaven when he commits suicide because he will have died with an unconfessed sin in his life.

Before we can deal with the subject of suicide among Christians, I believe we need to recognize the Bible fact that one does not go to Heaven because he is sin-free; he does not go to Heaven because he is good enough, nor does he lose Heaven because he has committed certain sins. Heaven is not, nor will it ever be, earned by good works or the lack of bad works.

There are several passages of Scripture which reveal this truth to us. Bible truth makes clear just how undeserving we are of salvation.

We are not, nor will we ever be, good enough to go to Heaven based on our own good merits. God tells us that He does not consider anything we do on our own as being good. The Bible teaches us that apart from the Lord, we lack the ability to do anything good.

"As it is written, There is none righteous, no, not one:

"There is none that understandeth, there is none that seeketh after God.

"They are all gone out of the way, they are together become unprofitable; there is none that doeth good, no, not one."—Rom. 3:10–12.

If you think your goodness will impress God,

then you are sadly mistaken. He has declared that apart from Him, you have yet to do one thing good. Even your personal righteousness is unacceptable to God. "But we are all as an unclean thing, and all our righteousnesses are as filthy rags" (Isa. 64:6). In ourselves we have nothing of which to boast.

The reason we are unacceptable to God is that we have missed His standard of perfection (Rom. 3:23). God's standard of perfection is Himself. We have sinned already, thus falling short of His requirements for perfection. Even if you could live the rest of your life without sin, you could not undo the sin you have already committed. You have already committed enough sin to doom you to a Devil's Hell. You have already missed the mark of God's glory. You are already guilty of breaking the law of God.

To commit just one offense is to be guilty of breaking the whole law of God. You are a lawbreaker; you are guilty before God of breaking His law. "For whosoever shall keep the whole law, and yet offend in one point, he is guilty of all" (Jas. 2:10).

In the fact of sin, all are as guilty as the suicides. Any sin is bad enough to warrant the death of the innocent Lamb of God. All sin carries the death penalty. "For the wages of sin is death; but the gift of God is eternal life through Jesus Christ our Lord" (Rom. 6:23).

Jesus Christ came to pay the penalty for our sin. He was the only one who could meet God's standard of perfection. "For he hath made him to be sin for us, who knew no sin; that we might be made the righteousness of God in him" (II Cor. 5:21). Jesus does not know what it is to commit even one sin; though tempted, He never once yielded to that temptation. "For we have not an high priest which cannot be touched with the feeling of our infirmities; but was in all points tempted like as we are, yet without sin" (Heb. 4:15). This is what made His sacrifice acceptable to God, while our righteousnesses remain an unacceptable sacrifice.

We are not saved by keeping the law, and we have already broken that law; and we are not kept saved by keeping the law.

"Therefore by the deeds of the law there shall no flesh be justified in his sight: for by the law is the knowledge of sin" (Rom. 3:20). The purpose of the law of God is to show us how sinful we already are, not to show us how sinless we are to become.

"For by grace are ye saved through faith; and that not of yourselves: it is the gift of God:

"Not of works, lest any man should boast."— Eph. 2:8,9.

The Lord has determined that salvation is by grace alone. Are there any sinners too wicked for the Lord to forgive and save? Is there enough grace to save any who call on the Lord?

"Moreover the law entered, that the offense might abound. But where sin abounded, grace did much more abound."—Rom. 5:20.

"All we like sheep have gone astray; we have turned every one to his own way; and the LORD hath laid on him the iniquity of us all."—Isa. 53:6.

When Jesus died on the cross, all the sins of mankind were placed on Him. He paid the penalty required for every sin and sinner. God's grace is great enough to save us from all sin. The greater the sin, the greater the grace.

Many people view salvation as a starting over. They think salvation is a cleaning of the slate, a cleansing from all past sin, and that now that they are clean, it is up to them to keep themselves clean or lose the salvation they have been granted. In other words, they believe they must keep themselves saved.

Suicide, then, would be a sin that would necessitate God's taking their salvation, once granted by grace, from them. They believe they would lose the right to be saved. This seems reasonable to many people, even some Christians; but is this taught in scripture?

The Bible teaches that when a person is saved, he is forgiven of all his sins.

"Be it known unto you therefore, men and brethren,

*that through this man is preached unto you the for-
giveness of sins:*

*"And by him all that believe are justified from all
things, from which ye could not be justified by the law
of Moses."*—Acts 13:38,39.

*"In whom we have redemption through his blood,
the forgiveness of sins, according to the riches of his
grace."*—Eph. 1:7.

The Bible teaches us that when we trust Christ
as Saviour, not only are we forgiven, but we are
also separated from our sins. "As far as the east is
from the west, so far hath he removed our transgressions from us" (Ps. 103:12). Therefore, when a
person is saved, his sins are removed from his
record forevermore. "For I will be merciful to their
unrighteousness, and their sins and their iniquities will I remember no more" (Heb. 8:12). Once
we are forgiven, our sins are forgotten.

But what happens if a person sins after salvation? Are those sins already forgiven, as far as
salvation is concerned?

*"Even as David also describeth the blessedness of the
man, unto whom God imputeth righteousness without
works,*

*"Saying, Blessed are they whose iniquities are for-
given, and whose sins are covered.*

*"Blessed is the man to whom the Lord will not
impute sin."*—Rom. 4:6–8.

Once saved, we are not only forgiven of our sins, but no other sin will ever be imputed to us. The word impute means "to account, to take an inventory, to add to one's account." When the Lord saves a person, he will never lose his salvation because of sin, for no sin can ever again be laid to his charge.

Is suicide a sin? The answer is yes. Since no sin is imputed to the Christian as far as salvation is concerned, then in that regard suicide is not imputed to his charge.

Does this mean that a Christian gets away with sin? Does this mean that Christians can sin and not have to worry about any consequences? The answer to this is an emphatic no. The nature of God is such that He will not let sin, even in the lives of His children, go unchecked. God has taken care of the penalty of sin, but He does not ignore the sins of His children. Your sins may be forgiven, but that does not mean there are no repercussions from your sin.

The Lord is too holy, too righteous and too just to allow sin to go on without doing something to stop it. The Lord will do whatever is necessary to prevent and stop His children from committing sin. The Bible calls it "chastisement." According to Hebrews, chapter 12, all of God's children are chastened of God. If they are not, they are not His children. The Lord is our Heavenly Father; therefore, He will treat us like any good father would treat a disobedient child.

What about the one who commits suicide? What will God do to the Christian who does such a thing? Since he does not have to worry about losing his salvation, then would it not be better to go ahead and commit suicide, get the problems behind him and enjoy the pleasures of Heaven?

Suicide will only catapult your problems on into eternity with you. The thought generally is that when you die, you leave all the problems behind; but suicide not only follows you into eternity, it takes with it the problems it produces as well.

"And I heard a voice from heaven saying unto me, Write, Blessed are the dead which die in the Lord from henceforth: Yea, saith the Spirit, that they may rest from their labours; and their works do follow them" (Rev. 14:13). The idea that suicide will end the problem is not true; it just increases the problem. When either a Christian or a lost person dies, his life is not left behind; rather, it goes with him. There is a difference, of course, between the final destinations of the saved and the lost, but the life each lived will follow him into eternity.

To understand this, we must look at some basic truths for all people, saved or unsaved. We all must appear before the Lord. "And as it is appointed unto men once to die, but after this the judgment" (Heb. 9:27). Death will end our earthly lives, but there is an eternal life for the saved and an eternal dying for the lost. The things we do here on earth have an impact on what takes place after our physical death. We, both the Christian and the lost person, will give an account of ourselves before God.

"For it is written, As I live, saith the Lord, every knee shall bow to me, and every tongue shall confess to God.

"So then every one of us shall give account of himself to God."—Rom. 14:11, 12.

Every person who has lived or who will ever live must give an account to God for what he did or did not do while here on earth.

What about the Christian who commits suicide? What will happen to him? Many Christians believe that once this life is over, they will live on easy street. They believe that their hard times will be left behind.

"And God shall wipe away all tears from their eyes; and there shall be no more death, neither sorrow, nor crying, neither shall there be any more pain: for the former things are passed away.

"And he that sat upon the throne said, Behold, I make all things new."—Rev. 21:4, 5.

We love to think of the time when there will be no more tears, pain, sorrow or death. We love to think of the street of gold and the never-ending joys of Heaven. But Revelation, chapter 21, takes place after the Tribulation, the judgment seat of

Christ, the millennial kingdom, the great white throne judgment and the creation of a new heaven and a new earth. This is after Satan is cast into the bottomless pit. If Jesus were to return for His children even as you read this sentence, there would still be one thousand seven years before we would come to what takes place in Revelation 21.

The Bible teaches that not every Christian will be happy when he sees the Lord. There will be some who will be ashamed when they see Jesus. "And now, little children, abide in him; that, when he shall appear, we may have confidence, and not be ashamed before him at his coming" (I John 2:28). There are Christians who will have to hang their heads in shame when they stand before God. They will not enjoy that first look at Jesus because they will not be ready to meet Him.

One reason they will be ashamed of themselves as they stand before God is that Jesus will be ashamed of them. When they see Jesus, they will see His disappointment in them. They will realize just how much they have let Him down. "Whosoever therefore shall be ashamed of me and of my words in this adulterous and sinful generation; of him also shall the Son of man be ashamed, when he cometh in the glory of his Father with the holy angels" (Mark 8:38).

The word ashamed used in this verse means "to feel shame for something." Can you imagine Jesus, your Saviour, being ashamed of you? The fact that you cause Jesus to feel ashamed of you will bring shame to you. When you see the disappointment of the One who died for you, saved you when you called on Him, watched over you and brought you to Heaven, you will not shout for joy. You will regret everything you have ever done that would cause Jesus to feel shame when He sees you. You will wish you could take back every such moment, action or deed. You will wish you had paid any price asked in service to Him, rather than to have made excuses for not serving Him.

When a Christian stands before God after having committed suicide, he will see his Heavenly Father ashamed of him because he doubted Him. The Bible teaches that the Lord has more for us than we can possibly imagine. "But as it is written, Eye hath not seen, nor ear heard, neither have entered into the heart of man, the things which God hath prepared for them that love him" (I Cor. 2:9). When we get to Heaven we will see firsthand the depth of the love the Lord has for us. Only then will we begin to comprehend just what we have in Christ. When a Christian who has committed suicide sees His glory, His power and His love, he will wonder how he could have so easily doubted Him. When he sees His power, he will wonder just why he did not trust Him enough to take care of his problems. He will be ashamed that he did not trust Him, love Him and obey Him.

In a church in Michigan where I was the pastor,

there was a lady whose son became very rebellious. He would bully his mother in order to get his way. One day it was determined that the only thing left to do was to send him to a Christian boys' home. As I talked with that mother, I saw the love she had for her son; but on the same face where her love for her son shone, tears of shame flowed unhindered. She loved her son, but she was ashamed of the way he was living. This is the same way the Lord feels about many of His children.

There is yet another reason why a Christian ought not commit suicide. As God's child, the Christian will also stand before the Lord and give an account of himself. "For we must all appear before the judgment seat of Christ; that every one may receive the things done in his body, according to that he hath done, whether it be good or bad" (II Cor. 5:10). The idea that all will be forgotten when the Christian dies is not biblical. Our works will follow us into Heaven! The unsaved will stand before the Lord and give an account of themselves, and we who are saved will do the same. Our judgment will be to determine not punishment but rewards.

"Every man's work shall be made manifest: for the day shall declare it, because it shall be revealed by fire; and the fire shall try every man's work of what sort it is.

"If any man's work abide which he hath built thereupon, he shall receive a reward.

"If any man's work shall be burned, he shall suffer loss: but he himself shall be saved; yet so as by fire."— I Cor. 3:13–15.

This judgment will be to separate the works done for the Lord and the works done for self. The works done for the Lord will endure the fire of God's judgment. God will judge them based on right and wrong and on motives. The works done for the praise of men and for the satisfying of the flesh will be burned up. Only the works done for the Lord will be rewarded. These rewards will not be just for church work. They will be given to the fathers that raised their children for the Lord. They will be for the employee who did his job as a Christian is supposed to do his job. These rewards will be given to the person who lived as a Christian is supposed to live.

According to the Bible, there will be some Christians who will receive no rewards of any kind as they stand before the Lord. They will have wasted their lives on the things of the world and will have no rewards in Heaven. They will be saved, but with no rewards.

Not only will some find that no rewards have been earned, but others will lose what rewards they had earned. These rewards were earned and prepared to be given, but because of some sin the Christian committed, they will be taken away. "Look to yourselves, that we lose not those things which we have wrought, but that we receive a full reward" (II John 8). It is possible not to receive a full reward. It would be a shame to live a life laying up treasures in Heaven, only to lose them at the end of that life.

Just how does this happen? In one church where I served, there was a man who was a deacon, Sunday school teacher and a great example to all who knew him. He spent years serving the Lord, but he started to get involved with sin, and he dropped out of church. The sin began to grow worse, and eventually it became known that he was involved in some very serious immorality. When it looked like he would be going to jail, he committed suicide. He undid in sin what had taken him a lifetime to do for the Lord. When he faced the Lord, he did not do so with joy but with shame. The Lord was not pleased with him; He was ashamed of him. The rewards that he had laid up in Heaven were not given to him, for he had lost them.

Some might say, "Well, I don't need any rewards. Just being in Heaven is good enough for me." They might think this somehow sounds spiritual. They might even think it a mark of humility; but if a person will study the Scriptures, he will find such an attitude is abominable. How can any Christian be content just to be in Heaven and not have the rewards that the Lord has for those who follow Him? Anyone who believes this does not understand what the Bible teaches about rewards. Such a person sees only the rewards, not the purpose for them.

The Lord established a Bible principle to be followed:

"....for the labourer is worthy of his hire."—Luke 10:7.

"Let the elders that rule well be counted worthy of double honour, especially they who labour in the word and doctrine."—I Tim. 5:17.

"Render therefore to all their dues: tribute to whom tribute is due; custom to whom custom; fear to whom fear; honour to whom honour."—Rom. 13:7.

The Lord teaches that a laborer is worthy of his hire, and a faithful elder is worthy of double honor. He teaches that honor is to be given to whom it is due. The Lord put it in His Word, and He will not violate His Word. To say that you do not want any rewards would be to say that you do not want the Lord to bestow upon you what He has deemed your due. Not to have any rewards is to have done nothing worthy of reward. Do you really want to stand before the Lord and the hosts of Heaven having done nothing for the one who saved you?

What will we do with those rewards? The rewards are not for the rewards' sake. They are not so we can boast of our great accomplishments. "That no flesh should glory in his presence" (I Cor. 1:29). The Lord is opposed to pride and boasting.

The Lord will not allow the sin of pride in Heaven. What will we do with the rewards we have received in Heaven?

"The four and twenty elders fall down before him that sat on the throne, and worship him that liveth for ever and ever, and cast their crowns before the throne, saying,

"Thou art worthy, O Lord, to receive glory and honour and power: for thou hast created all things, and for thy pleasure they are and were created."—Rev. 4:10,11.

I believe when we get to Heaven and receive the rewards from our Lord, we will be overcome with a gratitude such as we have yet to experience. When we see the love, the majesty, the beauty and the holiness of God, we will be so overcome with gratitude, we will want to give the Lord something to show our gratitude. All we will have in Heaven will have been provided for us by His grace. The only things we will have that will be returnable will be the rewards we have received from the Lord. To show our love for Him, we will cast our crowns at His feet in worship. Not to have any crowns is to have nothing to give back to the Lord. He, as well as we ourselves, will be ashamed of us; and we will have nothing by which to show the Lord how much we appreciate Him.

What a sad thing to be surrounded by the saints of old as they give to the Lord their tokens of love, and to have to kneel with bowed head but empty hands. What a sad thing to kneel before God after having died doubting His love, His provisions and His wisdom. Commit suicide, and you lose much of your joy in Glory. Commit suicide, and you will stand before the hosts of Heaven having doubted the very God who sits before you in all the splendor of Heaven. It is one thing to have to deal with them here on earth, but you will have allowed your problems to follow you to Heaven, because there you will suffer shame and loss of rewards. Do not allow your situation to rob you of your life, your rewards and the joy of giving to the Lord your tokens of love and appreciation.

Another sad thing about the Christians who take their own lives will be the sorrow they will feel as they watch the lost stand condemned before the Lord. I believe all the saints of heaven will be present as the Lord hands out the punishment of the lost. I believe we will see the condemned sentenced to an eternity in the lake of fire. Saved ones who committed suicide will watch as those who used them as an excuse not to get saved are cast into Hell. They will see those to whom they could have witnessed. They might have been the very ones who could have won certain lost ones, but they were so absorbed in self that they failed to do so.

They will also see Christians who followed their bad example or were otherwise led astray by the suicide: they were offended, they were devastated, they were hindered because a Christian friend or acquaintance committed suicide. Now they stand before the Lord empty-handed. Not only does the Christian suicide rob himself of the opportunity to cast crowns at Jesus' feet, but he may also influence fellow-Christians to the extent that they too will lose rewards. There will be so much shame.

Christian, you are hurting right now, and you see no way past your situation. You are helpless, hopeless, filled with sorrow of heart, and you are weary with life. You see nothing for which to live. You think you may want to end your life, but keep on reading because the story is not finished. There are some real answers for you in the Word of God.

Do not let the Devil convince you that suicide is the best way out. The only thing suicide will do is to intensify and add to problems for you as well as for those left behind. Deal with the situation here and do not take it into eternity with you. You will lose some things in eternity because of suicide. It will follow you, rob you and diminish your future joy. It will be on your mind beyond the grave, though eventually God will wipe away all tears from your eyes.

Chapter 6

HOPE FOR THOSE CONTEMPLATING SUICIDE

If we are to help someone who is contemplating suicide, we must give to him something besides our opinion. He must have something that has stood the test of time, and that is the Bible.

The Lord created man and gave him life. Jesus said He came to give life and to give it more abundantly. The Lord knows what is needed to make life work. Man's problem is that he keeps trying to improve on God's method. He wants life to work apart from God, so he replaces Bible truth with human reasoning, then wonders why it doesn't work.

What hope can we give to someone who has gone beyond helplessness, hopelessness, and sorrow of heart and has reached the point of weariness of life? Is there anything we can say or offer to someone in this condition?

Several things in the Bible offer hope to the otherwise helpless, hopeless, sorrowful, weary person.

Salvation

Many people blame God for their situation, but they have never done one thing for Him. They have been busy living life to its fullest. Now they find themselves in a situation that leaves them with no one to whom to turn.

The first place for them to begin the search for answers is in the Lord and the salvation He offers.

When the Philippian jailer awoke to find the prison doors open, he was ready to take his own life. He was afraid all the prisoners had escaped; however, when he saw that his fears had not been realized, he knew immediately what he needed. His life had been spared by the intervention of the Apostle Paul; now, rather than taking his life, he reached for eternal life. Rather than taking his life, he was born again.

"And the keeper of the prison awaking out of his sleep, and seeing the prison doors open, he drew out his sword, and would have killed himself, supposing that the prisoners had been fled.

"But Paul cried with a loud voice, saying, Do thyself no harm: for we are all here.

"Then he called for a light, and sprang in, and came trembling, and fell down before Paul and Silas,

"And brought them out, and said, Sirs, what must I do to be saved?"—Acts 16:27–30.

The imprisonment of Paul and the earthquake that followed were not for Paul's sake but for the sake of the jailer. The Lord used the situation to bring him to the point where he was willing to be saved.

History is filled with those who have tried to live apart from the Lord. Ever since the Fall of man in the Garden of Eden, he has attempted to live by his own code of ethics. The Tower of Babel mentioned in Genesis 11 is just one example of early man's trying to build his own religious code.

No matter how much we try, we cannot escape the fact that man was not made to live apart from the Lord. One reason such a life is a failure is that life does not end at death. If there were nothing *after* death, we would have little to fear *in* death.

After death comes eternity. Since there is an eternity, there is a real need for the Lord. He is the only One who can give us eternal life.

Until we see the real value of the human soul, we will never see the importance of salvation, and salvation will be nothing more than a word. The One who gives eternal life to man is also the One who knows the best way for this life to be lived.

I have seen people living to fulfill their own wants and desires. This results in a life of helplessness and hopelessness. The end result of a self-centered life is always despair. Many must reach this point, however, before they are willing to turn to the Lord. Sometimes even when people acknowledge the Lord to some extent, they attempt to regulate Him, not seeming to realize that the way they have chosen to live is what has caused the dilemma in which they find themselves.

The success or failure of a life is determined by one's choices and actions. We ought not be surprised when things do not work out when we have lived our lives apart from the will of God.

"There is a way which seemeth right unto a man, but the end thereof are the ways of death."—Prov. 14:12.

"Good understanding giveth favour: but the way of transgressors is hard."—Prov. 13:15.

For years man has tried to prove the Lord wrong, but he has always failed. Sometimes it is not until things fall apart that people are willing to come to the Lord. They wait until it is too late to learn that life really begins with Jesus.

The solution to any problem begins with salvation. Without salvation you have one very big problem—the loss of your eternal soul. Without salvation, you are destined to live your life without the Lord. Without salvation, you have no person to whom to go in prayer. Without salvation, you have nothing for which to hope, for at death all chances for anything better end.

Man is born a sinner. "Behold, I was shapen in iniquity; and in sin did my mother conceive me" (Ps. 51:5). Because of this sin nature, mankind sins. "Wherefore, as by one man sin entered into the world, and death by sin; and so death passed upon all men, for that all have sinned" (Rom. 5:12). No one except the Lord Jesus Christ Himself has ever lived a life apart from sin. Ever since Adam, man has not only been born a sinner but has been guilty of committing sin. "For all have sinned, and come short of the glory of God" (Rom. 3:23). Because of this sin, God had to separate Himself from man. His holiness cannot allow sin to be ignored or forgotten; so all sin, no matter how seemingly insignificant, must be paid for.

God stated the payment in the Garden of Eden: "But of the tree of the knowledge of good and evil, thou shalt not eat of it: for in the day that thou eatest thereof thou shalt surely die" (Gen. 2:17).

Many like to think God is too loving to send anyone to a place of torment, but He does not use human logic to determine His character. "Behold, all souls are mine; as the soul of the father, so also the soul of the son is mine: the soul that sinneth, it shall die" (Ezek. 18:4). It is because of God's character that He placed the price on sin. "For the wages of sin is death; but the gift of God is eternal life through Jesus Christ our Lord" (Rom. 6:23).

This death is "the second death" of Revelation 21:8: "But the fearful, and unbelieving, and the abominable, and murderers, and whoremongers, and sorcerers, and idolaters, and all liars, shall have their part in the lake which burneth with fire and brimstone: which is the second death."

This death is in the place of torment spoken of in Luke 16:23: "And in hell he lift up his eyes, being in torments, and seeth Abraham afar off, and Lazarus in his bosom."

Hell is a place of pain and torment which will last for all eternity. "And the smoke of their torment ascendeth up for ever and ever: and they have no rest day nor night, who worship the beast and his image, and whosoever receiveth the mark of his name" (Rev. 14:11).

No rest, no peace, no comfort await those who are not saved.

Is your belief about Hell different from what the Bible says? If it is, are you willing to chance your eternity on your opinion, ignoring God's Word?

How can God be loving and send someone to Hell? True love never excuses or overlooks sin and wrong. "He that spareth his rod hateth his son: but he that loveth him chasteneth him betimes" (Prov. 13:24). The love of God paid the price for our sin. "Herein is love, not that we loved God, but that he loved us, and sent his Son to be the propitiation for our sins" (I John 4:10). There is no greater love than that of one who lays down his life for others.

Jesus died as a substitute for others. His death was to prevent them from having to die for their sins. The love of the Lord goes a step further:

"For scarcely for a righteous man will one die: yet peradventure for a good man some would even dare to die.

"But God commendeth his love toward us, in that,

while we were yet sinners, Christ died for us."—
Rom. 5:7,8.

If we were called on to die for another, we might do so if we loved him and if he were a righteous man. But Jesus died for the worst of men, as if He were guilty of committing every sin that would ever be committed. The sins of all mankind were placed on Him, thus making His death a valid payment for our sin. This is a love far beyond the love expressed by man.

With sin's debt paid, salvation is offered to all men; all that remains is to receive it.

"That if thou shalt confess with thy mouth the Lord Jesus, and shalt believe in thine heart that God hath raised him from the dead, thou shalt be saved.

"For with the heart man believeth unto righteousness; and with the mouth confession is made unto salvation....

"For whosoever shall call upon the name of the Lord shall be saved."—Rom. 10:9,10,13.

This salvation is offered by grace through faith, not as a reward for your good works. After all, what have we ever done that could be compared to what Jesus has done for us? If you are to be saved, it will not be by your merit or good works. Only Jesus who took your guilt can save your soul. Your part is to admit your guilt and accept Him as your personal Saviour. He will save you from Hell if you will let Him.

If you have not accepted Him, you can do so now. If you are ready to be saved, simply pray to the Lord a prayer similar to this:

> Dear Lord Jesus, I know I have sinned against You and deserve to go to Hell. I believe when You died on the cross, You died for my sin. I believe You rose from the dead and are in Heaven with the Father. The best I know how, I ask You to forgive me of my sins and come into my heart and life. Please take me to Heaven when I die. Thank You for loving me and saving me. In Your name I ask this. Amen.

Once you put your faith and trust in the Lord, you become His child. "But as many as received him, to them gave he power to become the sons of God, even to them that believe on his name" (John 1:12). This makes the Lord your Heavenly Father. Thus, He becomes the One to whom you can flee in time of trouble (Ps. 121:1,2).

Until the matter of your salvation is settled, you have no claim on the Lord.

If you are dealing with someone contemplating suicide, you must take care of the spiritual need before you can offer him any hope. After his salvation is dealt with, you can start eliminating the individual steps to suicide. You can offer him hope from God's Word for each of his problems.

Many Things in Life Are Beyond Our Control

Many things about ourselves are beyond our control. "Which of you by taking thought can add one cubit unto his stature?" (Matt. 6:27). Where we were born, to whom we were born, and when we were born were all beyond our control. Where we grew up, with whom we grew up, and how we grew up were also out of our control. We cannot control our height, the aging process or most of the circumstances in which we find ourselves. Most of a person's life is really out of his control. The secret to life is not in controlling the situation but in dealing with the situation.

We also cannot control the day in which we live. "Take therefore no thought for the morrow: for the morrow shall take thought for the things of itself. Sufficient unto the day is the evil thereof" (Matt. 6:34). We cannot control tomorrow, nor did we control yesterday; so why do we think we ought to control today? The day is what it is—be it good or bad. Bad things happen to both the good and the bad. "That ye may be the children of your Father which is in heaven: for he maketh his sun to rise on the evil and on the good, and sendeth rain on the just and on the unjust" (Matt. 5:45). Every person on Planet Earth is in the same situation in which you find yourself today—having to deal with circumstances beyond his control. Be it good or bad, right or wrong, fair or unjust, we are controlled mostly by someone or something else. If you are having a bad day, just keep looking to the Lord and trusting Him. Remember, most of your life is spent dealing with things that are beyond your control.

The Lord, however, *is* in control.

"Trust in the LORD with all thine heart; and lean not unto thine own understanding.

"In all thy ways acknowledge him, and he shall direct thy paths."—Prov. 3:5, 6.

We like to think of ourselves as great stewards of wisdom. We think our perception is so in-depth that it must be right, but only One really knows all the facts and figures. Faith is simply obedience, leaving the results with the Lord. Obey His leading and leave the results with Him.

As you trust Him, keep this in mind: your help comes from Him. It may not be in the form you want, but if you are to receive help, it must come from Him.

"I will lift up mine eyes unto the hills, from whence cometh my help.

"My help cometh from the LORD, which made heaven and earth."—Ps. 121:1, 2.

The One who is in control is the only real help we have. Many times it looks like He has abandoned us, but our "help cometh from the LORD." We must simply trust Him.

As we trust Him, we must realize that His perspective is the only true one. Learn to trust His judgment. "For as the heavens are higher than the earth, so are my ways higher than your ways, and my thoughts than your thoughts" (Isa. 55:9). We do not see all that He sees; we do not know all He knows. What we must do, then, is trust the character of the One who sees all, of Him who promised to give us what we need in order to endure the situation.

"And lest I should be exalted above measure through the abundance of the revelations, there was given to me a thorn in the flesh, the messenger of Satan to buffet me, lest I should be exalted above measure.

"For this thing I besought the Lord thrice, that it might depart from me.

"And he said unto me, My grace is sufficient for thee: for my strength is made perfect in weakness. Most gladly therefore will I rather glory in my infirmities, that the power of Christ may rest upon me.

"Therefore I take pleasure in infirmities, in reproaches, in necessities, in persecutions, in distresses for Christ's sake: for when I am weak, then am I strong."—II Cor. 12:7–10.

For some reason the Lord knew you needed the particular burden of this day, so He allowed it to be placed upon you. The Lord does not ask you to carry it alone; allow Him to carry it for you. It is His grace that will get you through today, then tomorrow. Simply obey Him and entrust the results to Him.

The Solution to Your Problem May Not Be Deliverance From It

The solution may not be deliverance from the problem but contentment in the midst of it. The Lord said that His grace is sufficient for us. He is saying that the grace He gives during hard times may be all we are going to receive.

The word *sufficient* has several meanings: "adequate for contentment," "to be enough." What He gives to help us endure the situation is enough. We are to be content with that, for He may not remove the problem. Often for reasons known only to Him, we need this "thorn" in our lives, and we need His grace more than deliverance from the "thorn."

This is where trust comes in. Do we trust the Lord enough to accept His answer?

Paul sought deliverance from his thorn in the flesh; he was denied. The children of Israel sought deliverance from their bondage in Egypt; they received it after several hundred years in bondage. It took eighty of those years to prepare Moses to be their deliverer. Did the Lord fail Paul? Was the Lord not being fair to Paul? Paul knew the reason.

"But after long abstinence Paul stood forth in the

midst of them, and said, Sirs, ye should have hearkened unto me, and not have loosed from Crete, and to have gained this harm and loss.

"And now I exhort you to be of good cheer: for there shall be no loss of any man's life among you, but of the ship.

"For there stood by me this night the angel of God, whose I am, and whom I serve,

"Saying, Fear not, Paul; thou must be brought before Cæsar: and, lo, God hath given thee all them that sail with thee.

"Wherefore, sirs, be of good cheer: for I believe God, that it shall be even as it was told me.

"Howbeit we must be cast upon a certain island."—
Acts 27:21–26.

Paul did not question the Lord; he trusted Him. He did not seek deliverance from the situation but contentment in the situation. A promise from the Lord was all he needed.

The one thing people seek most is contentment. We are looking for that one thing, that certain possession, that certain amount of money, or that certain situation that says, "You have enough." One of the greatest treasures in this world is a contented life. "But godliness with contentment is great gain" (I Tim. 6:6). Paul knew this great Bible truth.

"Not that I speak in respect of want: for I have learned, in whatsoever state I am, therewith to be content.

"I know both how to be abased, and I know how to abound: every where and in all things I am instructed both to be full and to be hungry, both to abound and to suffer need.

"I can do all things through Christ which strengtheneth me."—Phil. 4:11–13.

He did not get his contentment in deliverance but in what the Lord saw as the supply of his real need at the time. He learned to be content in whatever the Lord deemed sufficient.

Many times we see deliverance as the only solution to our problems. It may be, however, the solution is to find what you need *in* the situation, not deliverance *from* the situation. It may be the Lord wants you to trust Him during the problems. We must trust the Lord while in need as well as when abounding.

The fact that the Lord has not given you what you think you need does not mean He has failed you. There is light at the end of the tunnel. Your need is to pray for grace and contentment on your way to that light.

The psalmist expressed it so beautifully in Psalm 23:4: "Yea, though I walk through the valley of the shadow of death, I will fear no evil: for thou art with me; thy rod and thy staff they comfort me." The comfort of the rod and staff came while *in* the valley. The comfort you need in your circumstances must come from the Lord.

As Long As the Lord Is on His Throne, There Is Hope

Many times we see ourselves as facing the impossible. We see no way out, nor do we foresee ever finding any way out. The truth is, often there is no way out. When someone dies or when a person loses everything by some catastrophe and there seems to be no answer to the situation, we conclude that there is no hope. But to say there is no hope is to say there is no God. Our hope may come in a form different than we expect, but there is hope.

A great example is when someone is diagnosed with a terminal illness. We think the hope is in the cure. It may be that the hope is in the grace the Lord gives during the illness. The hope is not dependent upon a cure. Hope did not die with the doctor's diagnosis nor with the impossibility of a cure. There is always hope with the Lord.

This is not to say a person does not suffer. This is not saying we are to be "on top of the world" at all times. But we should realize there is always hope.

When it came to hardship, King David had this to say: "Why art thou cast down, O my soul? and why art thou disquieted within me? hope thou in God: for I shall yet praise him, who is the health of my countenance, and my God" (Ps. 42:11). At the time of the writing of this psalm, David was disquieted, cast down, depressed and in an uproar.

He was "eaten up" on the inside while he was downtrodden by all that was happening to him. He was not "on top of the world," nor was he praising God; but he could hope in the Lord because he knew the time would come when he would be able to praise God again.

Your being down now doesn't mean you will always be down. Your not being able to see the solution now does not mean there isn't one. Sure, it hurts now; sure, it hurts too badly to praise the Lord now; but the story is not over yet.

The Apostle Paul was also familiar with this truth: "And we know that all things work together for good to them that love God, to them who are the called according to his purpose" (Rom. 8:28).

"How can God bring good out of this situation?" we may ask. We may not know until we get to Heaven just what good this situation might have brought about, but the Lord is "able to do exceeding abundantly above all that we ask or think, according to the power that worketh in us" (Eph. 3:20). We are not able to get good out of it, but our weaknesses do not limit the Lord's power. It is His power, not ours, that He uses to do His will. "Blessed be the Lord, that hath given rest unto his people Israel, according to all that he promised: there hath not failed one word of all his good promise, which he promised by the hand of Moses his servant" (I Kings 8:56). He never promises anything that He does not have the power to fulfill. If the fulfillment requires a miracle, then expect a miracle!

Get Your Eyes on the Needy

Sometimes a person finds himself in such a terrible position that he feels everyone would be better off if he were dead. Many times, especially with a terminal illness, a person sees no reason to live. He sees himself as a burden on others. He sees nothing ahead that is encouraging so concludes that the next step is suicide.

For the Christian, death is the step into Heaven. The Apostle Paul knew what hardship was all about. Very few carry the battle scars that Paul carried.

"Are they ministers of Christ? (I speak as a fool) I am more; in labours more abundant, in stripes above measure, in prisons more frequent, in deaths oft.

"Of the Jews five times received I forty stripes save one.

"Thrice was I beaten with rods, once was I stoned, thrice I suffered shipwreck, a night and a day I have been in the deep;

"In journeyings often, in perils of waters, in perils of robbers, in perils by mine own countrymen, in perils by the heathen, in perils in the city, in perils in the wilderness, in perils in the sea, in perils among false brethren;

"In weariness and painfulness, in watchings often, in hunger and thirst, in fastings often, in cold and nakedness.

"Beside those things that are without, that which

cometh upon me daily, the care of all the churches."—II Cor. 11:23–28.

Death was definitely better for him, but listen to what he said:

"For I am in a strait betwixt two, having a desire to depart, and to be with Christ; which is far better:

"Nevertheless to abide in the flesh is more needful for you."—Phil. 1:23, 24.

It was better for him that he die, but better for others that he live. Paul's desire for death was not motivated by his desire to escape his hardships but rather to enjoy the pleasures of Heaven.

There is no fear in death, for Heaven is our reward. How could a child of the Lord dread going to Heaven? Salvation takes the fear out of death. There is no more sting in death. So to die and go on to Heaven is preferable, especially when compared to a life of pain.

But we must remember this great truth: We are not left here for our own betterment. It was better for Paul that he die but more needful for others that he live. Get your eyes off what is *better* for you and get them on the *need.* Quit looking at yourself and start looking at the needs of others. Your purpose in life is not to achieve your own comfort level nor your own desires, but to fulfill the Lord's purpose for your being here. As long as there are lost souls to be won, needs to be met, jobs to be done, a testimony to be given, then there is a need for you.

It is time to get your eyes off yourself and on the Lord. "...not as I will, but as thou wilt" (Matt. 26:39). Jesus sought only the will of the Lord. Is that your same desire? We should not want our will, but His, to be done. It is God's will for you to be alive. That is why you have not been taken in death; that is why you have not been removed from your trying situation. Since it is the Lord's will for you to live under these circumstances, then why are you contemplating suicide? Once dead, you will have no opportunity to be a blessing to others.

You might be in serious pain and wonder how your life could be in anyone's best interest, but that is not for you to determine. We have no right to play God. We are His, and He is in control. Do not attempt to take the controls from Him. There is no person any better equipped than the Lord to whom to entrust your life. No one can help you live it any better than the One who gave it to you. Trust Him to work out what He deems as needful, not what you think is needful.

The Lord May Have Ordained for You to Go Through This Situation

Many times the seemingly impossible situations are needful. There are many verses in the Bible that teach this great truth. One is Psalm

119:71: "It is good for me that I have been afflicted; that I might learn thy statutes." Some of life's most important lessons are learned by going through affliction. An example is what the Lord has to do to get us to pray. Often He has to put us in situations beyond our own ability to handle in order to get us to come to Him. Sometimes we face illness so we can learn to trust Him. We go through hardship so that we can be used later on to help others.

"Blessed be God, even the Father of our Lord Jesus Christ, the Father of mercies, and the God of all comfort;

"Who comforteth us in all our tribulation, that we may be able to comfort them which are in any trouble, by the comfort wherewith we ourselves are comforted of God.

"For as the sufferings of Christ abound in us, so our consolation also aboundeth by Christ.

"And whether we be afflicted, it is for your consolation and salvation, which is effectual in the enduring of the same sufferings which we also suffer: or whether we be comforted, it is for your consolation and salvation."—II Cor. 1:3–6.

We must learn to find comfort in the Lord so that we can comfort others. Many hurting people need to trust the Lord in their times of trouble. How can we help them if we have not trusted Him during the problems we have faced?

No matter the reason for our circumstance, the

Lord knows about it and has His own purpose for what He does.

"But the Lord said unto him, Go thy way: for he is a chosen vessel unto me, to bear my name before the Gentiles, and kings, and the children of Israel:

"For I will shew him how great things he must suffer for my name's sake."—Acts 9:15, 16.

There is a comfort in knowing that there is a purpose in your suffering. These hardships that have brought you to the point of helplessness, hopelessness, sorrow of heart and weariness are not without a purpose. They are either for your benefit or the benefit of another; but if endured rightly, they will fulfill the Lord's purpose.

One of the reasons doctor-assisted suicide is wrong is that the good that can come out of suffering is removed. When Jesus walked on earth, He showed the disciples a blind man. They asked Him whose sin it was that caused this man to be born blind. This is the answer Jesus gave: "Neither hath this man sinned, nor his parents: but that the works of God should be made manifest in him" (John 9:3). Because of this man's blindness we, as well as the disciples and the people near, have been able to see the power of God.

We will never know till we get to Heaven how many people have been blessed by this Bible story. This blind man had spent a lifetime in darkness so Jesus could come by and heal him. All the suffering he went through because of his blindness was so that God could reveal His power through him in his adult years.

A personal example of this truth is my mother who died of cancer on June 27, 1989. She had been diagnosed with this terrible disease five years earlier. She didn't wait until she got cancer to get right with the Lord and start serving Him. As far back as I can remember, she had always served the Lord. She had a great testimony in both the church and the community.

When she found out she had cancer, it was a great shock to the whole family. Her mother had died of cancer when my mother was eighteen, so she knew firsthand the pain and torment of fighting this battle. But even during the thick of the battle when things were at their worst, she didn't let the cancer stop her. She used it and the discomfort of treatment as another way of serving the Lord.

Even during chemotherapy she didn't miss teaching her Sunday school class. Every service she would travel the eighteen miles to church, no matter what the weather or her health. She loved her church, her pastor and her Lord. My dad made the statement, "She was an even better Christian the last five years of her life than before."

It was her cancer that made her testimony stand out for the Lord.

Usually the stories that inspire us the most are the ones about people going through a great hardship. It is not the easy life that motivates us to do better; it is when great obstacles are overcome.

It may be that the Lord has chosen you to be a great example to others. You cannot be that example apart from hardship. The situation in which you find yourself today may be just what is needed to boost your testimony tomorrow. Serve the Lord, and others will be inspired by your devotion.

When a person commits suicide, he has eliminated his opportunity to be an example to others. He has removed the instrument through which the Lord would have revealed His glory. He has also hurt those who otherwise would have been inspired by his example. In many cases they may be his own family. All children need to see their parents going through some hard times. It gives them an example to follow when they have to face difficult situations.

Enduring hardships is neither popular nor enjoyable. The pain is there; the hurt is intense; but our eyes and thoughts are not to be on what is better for us but on what is more needful for others. This attitude comes from selfless living. It is the same attitude that Jesus showed to us.

"Let this mind be in you, which was also in Christ Jesus:

"Who, being in the form of God, thought it not robbery to be equal with God:

"But made himself of no reputation, and took upon him the form of a servant, and was made in the likeness of men:

"And being found in fashion as a man, he humbled himself, and became obedient unto death, even the death of the cross."—Phil. 2:5–8.

He left Heaven to suffer for us. Who has benefited the most from what Jesus did?

An example of love is one's dying for a friend. Another example of love is one's being willing to suffer for a friend. We are so concerned about ourselves and how life affects us, that we forget about what our life may mean to others. How much better it is to leave the next generation with an example of someone who stuck it out rather than someone who took what seemed to be the easy way out and thereby removed an example.

Your Help, Hope, Encouragement and Strength Come From the Lord

When we focus on our own inabilities, many times we cannot see any way out of our troubles. But help, hope, encouragement and strength come from the Lord. How we make it through what lies ahead is the Lord's responsibility. It is not for us to figure out, nor is it up to us to make it work.

He is the One who makes the solutions probable and possible. Our help comes from the Lord (Ps. 121:1,2).

Things often get out of control because we try to make it without His help. The Christian is never truly helpless. At times, however, it may seem as if the Lord is nowhere to be found, but be assured that He never leaves us nor forsakes us. The help may come in a form we do not recognize; nevertheless, it will come.

Not only our help but our hope is from the Lord. "To whom God would make known what is the riches of the glory of this mystery among the Gentiles; which is Christ in you, the hope of glory" (Col. 1:27). Jesus is not only the *source* of our hope; He *is* our hope—the assurance and confidence we have for eternity.

"And this is the confidence that we have in him, that, if we ask any thing according to his will, he heareth us:

"And if we know that he hear us, whatsoever we ask, we know that we have the petitions that we desired of him."—I John 5:14,15.

When we realize that the promises of the Lord are carried out by His power, how can we despair?

Jesus is also our encouragement. "And David was greatly distressed; for the people spake of stoning him, because the soul of all the people was grieved, every man for his sons and for his daughters: but David encouraged himself in the

LORD his God" (I Sam. 30:6). When David feared for his life, he found encouragement in the Lord.

The Lord gives us promises to claim and believe. What good are promises if they can be neither trusted nor believed? But the promises of God are trustworthy and ought to be believed. The future may be as bright as the promises of God, but if we do not accept them nor act upon them, how can those promises encourage us now? We can find courage to overcome discouragement, joy for sorrow, and peace for anxiety—all promised by God. Many times we just need someone to put his arm around us and tell us, "Everything will be all right." What better person to assure us of that than the Lord?

The Lord is also our strength. "But they that wait upon the LORD shall renew their strength; they shall mount up with wings as eagles; they shall run, and not be weary; and they shall walk, and not faint" (Isa. 40:31). We find not only mental and spiritual peace but also physical strength.

Elijah was at his wit's end, discouraged and hopeless. If the Lord would just take him! The Lord, however, was not done with Elijah; but before he could continue, he had to find strength.

"But he himself went a day's journey into the wilderness, and came and sat down under a juniper tree: and he requested for himself that he might die; and said, It

is enough; now, O LORD, take away my life; for I am not better than my fathers.

"And as he lay and slept under a juniper tree, behold, then an angel touched him, and said unto him, Arise and eat.

"And he looked, and, behold, there was a cake baken on the coals, and a cruse of water at his head. And he did eat and drink, and laid him down again.

"And the angel of the LORD came again the second time, and touched him, and said, Arise and eat; because the journey is too great for thee.

"And he arose, and did eat and drink, and went in the strength of that meat forty days and forty nights unto Horeb the mount of God."—I Kings 19:4–8.

His circumstances didn't change, but his attitude did. The journey he was about to take was greater than he had strength to endure. The strength he found was not within himself but from the Lord.

What exactly do we mean when we talk about receiving strength from the Lord? The word *strength* means "force." The Lord gives us the force needed to accomplish what we need to do. When we are filled with His Spirit He puts the force in what we are doing. He is making things work out. He is giving us the ability to do what needs to be done. It can be physical strength, like that of Samson, or mental strength, like He gave Paul in all his afflictions. It could be strength of character, like that of the three Hebrews who refused to bow to the Babylonian king's image, thus placing themselves at death's door.

You may be facing the hardest time of your life, lacking the help, hope, encouragement and strength needed to carry you through. What you need can be found only in the Lord. He can give you guidance, strength and blessing. Let the Lord do that which only He can do. Simple obedience and trust are the pathway to answers.

Many people come to the end of themselves and think the only step left is suicide. They forget that when they have come to the end of their own way, they are only one step from the Lord. Many have been fooled into thinking, if they cannot do anything about the situation, neither can the Lord.

Often the Lord cannot do what needs to be done in our lives until we reach the place of great hardship. Not until we come to the end of ourselves can the Lord get glory from our lives. If He had sent the solution earlier, we would have said it was our abilities that brought deliverance. We should never think that.

Another Mission

One of the side effects of helplessness, hopelessness, sorrow of heart and weariness of life is the loss of vision. Everyone needs a vision, a mental image, a goal, a purpose for living. Proverbs 29:18 declares: "Where there is no vision, the people perish."

Loss of vision is seen among many who reach retirement age. Some of us know of those who have died shortly after retirement. Those who retire need some kind of work to do. Everyone needs a purpose for living.

The Prophet Elijah reached the point of lost vision. He said, "It is enough; now, O LORD, take away my life; for I am not better than my fathers." He had sacrificed for years, doing the Lord's work, only to see it seemingly fail. He was discouraged and despondent and saw no reason to continue. Nothing had changed or was likely to change in the near future. All he saw was more hiding, more sacrificing, more running. He thought there was nothing else for which to live.

But the Lord was not through with this prophet. Instead of giving up on Elijah, the Lord fed him and sent him to a cave, away from everything and everybody, where he could hear only the Lord speak. The Lord gave him another vision.

"And the LORD said unto him, Go, return on thy way to the wilderness of Damascus: and when thou comest, anoint Hazael to be king over Syria:

"And Jehu the son of Nimshi shalt thou anoint to be king over Israel: and Elisha the son of Shaphat of Abelmeholah shalt thou anoint to be prophet in thy room."—I Kings 19:15, 16.

There were two new kings to anoint and a new prophet to call. There were more of life to be lived by Elijah the prophet and more of the Lord's work to be done.

When you finally realize that the Lord is the One with the solution to your problem and you meet with Him, then you will find there is still more of life ahead. The Lord may have things for you to do of which you are not aware. You will find there are still reasons to get up in the morning, still a life to be lived, even if it is to be lived in affliction.

When the Lord is finished with you, He will take you out, but not until then. What you need is a new vision.

King Saul received a serious wound during his last battle. When he realized that the wound was fatal, he decided it would be better to die at his own hand than at the hands of the Philistines. What he should have done was pick up his sword and fight the Lord's enemy to the end. There were still a war going on and more enemies to fight.

Judas betrayed the Lord, then out of grief and guilt hung himself. What he should have done was to get saved and serve the Lord. There was enough of God's grace to save even Judas, had he called on Him for salvation.

The same is true with you. You may have lost your vision due to circumstances dealt you, but that doesn't mean there are no more visions. It doesn't mean that life is over. There is still more that you can and should do.

Moses was given seventy men to help with the burdens of leadership. It would have been a shame if Moses' life had ended when he prayed, "Kill me."

Things looked bleak for Jonah in the belly of the whale, but there was more ahead. He still had a city to reach.

The Philippian jailer, believing all his prisoners had escaped, may have seen no reason to continue living; but he had a family to get saved.

Even Job found a vision after the loss of his ten children, his possessions and his health. There were given to him ten more children and twice the amount of his former possessions.

There is always something else to be done. Your not being able to see beyond the moment does not mean there are no more visions. Right now you cannot see them, and if you turn to the Lord today, you may still not see them tomorrow. They may be revealed only one day at a time, and maybe not for several years yet.

The last chapter of your life is yet to be written. There may still be several chapters left to write. Why get discouraged and quit just before the last chapter? Maybe your whole life was lived for this very moment. Your greatest days may be ahead. Your greatest prayers may yet be prayed. Your greatest love may yet be given. Your greatest testimony may yet be seen. Why quit now just because you cannot see beyond the moment?

You may be seeing days ahead filled with pain or handicap. You may have lost your strength, your coordination, even your mobility. You may not be able to do anything without unbearable pain. You may be at the point where others must take care of you, and you despise the thought. But I assure you, there is still more of life ahead. The tasks that the Lord has given you now, no matter how meager, may be the most important of your life.

If all you can do is pray, than become the best prayer warrior you can possibly be. If all you can do is sit silently with your thoughts, the Lord knows about them. Learn to fellowship with Him. Let the Lord become your best friend. If others have to do things for you, maybe the Lord knows they need that experience in order to do more for Him in the future. Maybe the best thing you can give to your family is the opportunity to learn to live for others. After all, there is already enough selfishness in this world. One day all you will be on this earth is a memory, so make all the good memories you can for others. Suicide would be a mighty hard memory for your loved ones to live with.

What If It Does Not Get Any Better?

There is the possibility that your situation may

not get better. Maybe you will live with this hardship for the rest of your life. It might be that you are to suffer for the remainder of your days. Is there any purpose in a life of suffering? The Lord gives anyone in this condition a great promise to claim.

"Then answered Peter and said unto him, Behold, we have forsaken all, and followed thee; what shall we have therefore?

"And Jesus said unto them, Verily I say unto you, That ye which have followed me, in the regeneration when the Son of man shall sit in the throne of his glory, ye also shall sit upon twelve thrones, judging the twelve tribes of Israel.

"And every one that hath forsaken houses, or brethren, or sisters, or father, or mother, or wife, or children, or lands, for my name's sake, shall receive an hundredfold, and shall inherit everlasting life."— Matt. 19:27–29.

If you are called to a life of suffering and in it are faithful to the Lord, then the Lord will reward you accordingly. To whom much is given, of him much is required; of whom much is required, to him much will be rewarded.

If you will serve God, no matter what the cost, He will make sure your rewards are many times greater than any sacrifice you might have made.

Many will never receive their greatest possible rewards because they quit serving God when faced with their greatest difficulty. The greater the difficulty, the greater the opportunity to declare God faithful. The more you endure, the more grace you receive from the Lord.

The Decision

As Joshua approached the end of his life, he called all the leaders of Israel together and presented a challenge. He wanted to leave them with a few parting words to remind them that the Lord was the One who had given them the victory and the land to go with it. Therefore, they needed to put away the strange gods of the land and serve Him. He then told them of the decision they would have to make: "And if it seem evil unto you to serve the LORD, choose you this day whom ye will serve" (Josh. 24:15). God was Joshua's God, but was He Israel's God?

This is the decision you too must make. Whom are you going to serve? It matters little what anyone says to you if you are not willing to take his advice. You have been presented with what the Word of the Lord has to say, but it will do you no good unless you are willing to do what it says. You must choose for whom you will live your life. You can go ahead and do what you want, which is what has brought you to your helpless state. You can follow your own reasoning, which offers nothing but hopelessness. You can trust your own strength and strive to attain your own desires, which is what produced your sorrow of heart and weariness of life. You can continue to go the way you are going, or you can turn to the Lord who is our help, hope, encouragement and strength.

The choice is yours. One decision will produce an eternal reward and give your life some value. One decision will make this life of hardship worthwhile. You can go either the Lord's way or the wrong way. You can do either the Lord's will or the wrong will. You can do either the right thing or your own thing. The decision, the choice, the challenge, is yours.

Nothing can be done for you until you make the right decision. It is not something you try for a few days to see if it works out; it is a lifelong commitment. Perhaps the blessings will not come again until you get to Glory, but you must choose this day whom ye will serve. Whom will you choose? What will you choose?

Chapter 7

TO THOSE LEFT BEHIND

Whenever there is a suicide, those left behind will always suffer. Suicide is a selfish act by a self-centered person. The despair, depression and heartache are not over for the Christian who commits suicide (considering the judgment seat of Christ); and they are just beginning for the loved ones left behind on earth.

You may be suffering the aftermath of the suicide of a loved one. It may be *your* heart that is breaking, *your* mind that is confused. The guilt may be pricking your heart, and questions may be plaguing you. You may be the one crying yourself to sleep as you recall this terrible event.

Is there any hope for you? Can anything bring comfort to your broken heart? Let me share a few things with you.

It Is Supposed to Hurt

When a loved one dies, especially at his own hand, it hurts terribly. But be it understood that it is supposed to hurt. We are supposed to cry.

"To every thing there is a season, and a time to every purpose under the heaven...

"A time to weep, and a time to laugh; a time to mourn, and a time to dance."—Eccles. 3:1, 4.

The degree of pain is partially determined by the degree of love. People die every day. In any funeral home there probably are people who are sorrowing because a loved one has died. You can see their sorrow and not be stirred. You can go inside, stand by the casket, look on the face of the deceased and not be stirred. The reason is that there is no special love in your heart for that corpse. We weep only for those we love.

When you lose someone for whom you cared, the pain is real and seems unbearable. But the pain is supposed to be there. Many times we get a false idea of how things are supposed to be. Because we are Christians, we think we are supposed to be above heartache, pain and tears. But the Lord made us to hurt when there is cause for our hearts to be broken. We do not sorrow as those who have no hope, but the sorrow is there, and it is real. You need to understand that this sorrow you feel is natural. It is supposed to hurt.

The Suicide's Help Could Have Been Found in the Lord, Not in You

The aftermath of suicide usually includes guilt. People start thinking things like, *I should have noticed,* or *I should have done something.* A loved one or friend feels as if he is partly responsible for the tragedy. Often this guilt lasts for years, and in some cases, a lifetime.

I have talked with some whose loved ones have

committed suicide. Several seemed so full of guilt that I thought it would affect them the rest of their lives.

I know one man whose best friend committed suicide. He found the body. That suicide has been relived in his mind ever since, and he has not been the same.

If you are in a similar situation, I want to give you some Bible truths to help you face this sorrow. You must understand that the hope your loved one needed was not in you but in the Lord. You cannot do what only the Lord can do. The strength your loved one needed comes only from the Lord. Jeremiah 17:5 verifies that statement: "Cursed be the man that trusteth in man, and maketh flesh his arm."

When man trusts in man, he will be only as strong as the man in whom he is trusting. The strength your loved one needed could have come only from the Lord. The only real comfort we have to offer is that which we have received from the Lord.

"Blessed be God, even the Father of our Lord Jesus Christ, the Father of mercies, and the God of all comfort;

"Who comforteth us in all our tribulation, that we may be able to comfort them which are in any trouble, by the comfort wherewith we ourselves are comforted of God."—II Cor. 1:3, 4.

The Bible gives the message of comfort to those
who are suffering. It is a message of hope to the
hopeless, help to the helpless, and strength to the
weak. "Wherefore comfort one another with these
words" (I Thess. 4:18). It is not our words nor our
wisdom that touches hearts—we can touch only
the intellect. The Holy Spirit is the One who
touches the heart. He is the great Comforter, the
only One who can reach beyond the exterior,
beyond the problems, and into the very heart of
man. The Holy Spirit delivers the message that all
will be well. The best we can do is give out the
message of comfort that the Lord gives to us, then
let the Holy Spirit use it to touch hearts.

We must also realize that the choice of accept-
ing the Lord's help was the suicide's. We are told
in Revelation 3:20, "Behold, I stand at the door,
and knock: if any man hear my voice, and open the
door, I will come in to him, and will sup with him,
and he with me." The Lord does not force His
will on anyone, though He makes it available to
everyone. The Lord is not willing that any should
perish. The offer of help has been made, but in
order for that help to be beneficial, it must be
accepted. The Lord is willing to save any who call
upon Him, but He will not force His salvation or
help on anyone.

The Question of Guilt

The guilt felt by those who have lost a loved one

through suicide can be overwhelming. It points a finger of accusation and condemns us. It causes us to question ourselves and offers nothing in which to find rest. It causes us to sorrow far beyond the pain of lost love, and drives us to despair.

Is there any hope for those suffering from guilt?

The first thing of which to remind yourself is, if your loved one was not willing to accept the Lord's comfort, strength and help, what makes you think he would have accepted yours? There is nothing that anyone could have given that could have taken the place of the help offered by the Lord. There is no substitute for the Lord's wisdom, nor hope besides that given by Him. There is no strength, no help, no comfort apart from God.

If the one who committed suicide did accept the salvation offered, then his sins were forgiven when he put his trust in the Lord—even the sin of suicide.

Salvation is not selective of which sin is forgiven or is not forgiven. All sin—past, present and future—was paid for by Christ on the cross. All transgressions were placed on Him, and He paid for them in full. Once received, salvation makes it impossible for any sin to be held against the child of God.

"What shall we say then that Abraham our father, as pertaining to the flesh, hath found?

"For if Abraham were justified by works, he hath

whereof to glory; but not before God.

"For what saith the scripture? Abraham believed God, and it was counted unto him for righteousness.

"Now to him that worketh is the reward not reckoned of grace, but of debt.

"But to him that worketh not, but believeth on him that justifieth the ungodly, his faith is counted for righteousness.

"Even as David also describeth the blessedness of the man, unto whom God imputeth righteousness without works,

"Saying, Blessed are they whose iniquities are forgiven, and whose sins are covered.

"Blessed is the man to whom the Lord will not impute sin."—Rom. 4:1–8.

The word *imputeth* means "to charge to one's account." Once we are saved, the righteousness of Jesus is charged to our account, and our sins are placed on Him. Psalm 103:12 assures us, "As far as the east is from the west, so far hath he removed our transgressions from us." Once forgiven, our sins will be remembered no more. They will not be brought up at the judgment, for the punishment for them was already carried out on Calvary.

"But," you say, "is not suicide the same as self-murder?" It is self-murder, but salvation covers even murder. The Apostle Paul helped kill many Christians, yet salvation was given to him. King David had Uriah killed, yet we see salvation brought forgiveness to him. The greater the sin, the greater the grace to forgive it.

"For as by one man's disobedience many were made sinners, so by the obedience of one shall many be made righteous.

"Moreover the law entered, that the offence might abound. But where sin abounded, grace did much more abound:

"That as sin hath reigned unto death, even so might grace reign through righteousness unto eternal life by Jesus Christ our Lord."—Rom. 5:19–21.

There is no sin that was not paid for on Calvary. Therefore, salvation is for all who believe, no matter what their sin. Once salvation is received, it will never be taken away.

Some might look at this as a license to sin, but the Bible deals with this:

"What shall we say then? Shall we continue in sin, that grace may abound?

"God forbid. How shall we that are dead to sin, live any longer therein?"—Rom. 6:1,2.

The Christian who has reached the point of helplessness, hopelessness, sorrow of heart and weariness of life, and has ended his life with suicide, has not lost his salvation. He is in Heaven, though there he will probably suffer the loss of rewards. Loved ones left on earth can do nothing about a suicide's standing in eternity; therefore, they should appropriate the grace of God to alleviate their grief so that they can go on serving God.

Many times people will keep going over and over the suicide, looking for answers. Often anger sets in, resulting in a life of bitterness and sorrow.

There are those who let the suicide of a loved one control their whole lives. This need not be: there is comfort in Jesus. The deceased should have taken their problems to the Lord; those left behind need to do the same.

King David found himself in a place where his men spoke of killing him. His wife, as well as their wives, had been taken captive by an invading army. David did the only thing he could do: "David encouraged himself in the LORD" (I Sam. 30:6). His encouragement did not come from his own ability to "tough it out"—he had no ability to do so. He looked to the Lord to give him the courage needed to face the direst of circumstances.

Jesus has what you need to get through your grief over a loved one's suicide. He can touch your heart and give you peace. He feels your hurt and sorrow, and hurts with you, sorrows with you.

Here is a great truth for those who are saved yet suffering from the suicide of another. The Lord gives us a promise of hope for today and tomorrow: "To appoint unto them that mourn in Zion, to give unto them beauty for ashes, the oil of joy for mourning, the garment of praise for the spirit of heaviness" (Isa. 61:3).

Suicide is sin and proceeds from Satan, yet the Lord can bring to pass some good in spite of a suicide. The *how* is not as important as the fact that He *can* do it. Often we get so focused on the impossibility of the action needed that we forget we are dealing with an all-powerful God. We do not need to know the *how*—just the fact that He *can*.

"And this is the confidence that we have in him, that, if we ask any thing according to his will, he heareth us:

"And if we know that he hear us, whatsoever we ask, we know that we have the petitions that we desired of him."—I John 5:14, 15.

When we get to Heaven and there have the complete story, we may be able to see that some good was accomplished of which we never knew while on earth.

It is not God's will for a person to commit suicide, but He is capable of bringing something good out of a terrible tragedy. Only He can bring beauty out of ashes.

Chapter 8

HOW TO HELP THOSE CON-TEMPLATING SUICIDE OR THOSE SUFFERING BECAUSE OF IT

We have seen the attitudes that are typical of depressed people. Some such people may even commit suicide. We have looked at helplessness, hopelessness, sorrow of heart and weariness of life. We have seen the Bible truths that offer the solution to each of these attitudes. We have also looked at those suffering guilt in the aftermath of suicide.

But how can we help someone who is suicidal? How can we help those suffering from the suicide of a loved one? We do not want to sit back and say nothing. What can we do to make a difference for them?

Realize There Is Help, Hope, Comfort and Strength for Them. We need to be confident that the Lord has the solution to any hopeless situation. Even if they do not accept what we tell them, we ourselves must have confidence that the Lord has the answer for them. We must know it ourselves before we can convince others. Some will lean on our assurance. Those in grief need to see that we believe what we are saying and are not just parroting something we have heard or read.

Our Lord has the answer to every problem in life.

In Order to Offer Them a Saviour, We Ought to Be in Fellowship With That Saviour. Very few will listen to what we have to say unless we believe it enough to live it. Truth stated cannot do as much as truth lived. "Shew me thy faith without thy works, and I will shew thee my faith by my works" (Jas. 2:18).

Actions speak louder than words. Truth lived is more powerful than truth stated. Some people want help from the Lord without being right with the Lord. It will not work for them, nor will it work for you. If others are to listen to you, you must be in fellowship with the Lord.

Ask the Lord for Wisdom. James 1:5 states: "If any of you lack wisdom, let him ask of God, that giveth to all men liberally, and upbraideth not; and it shall be given him." The wisdom needed is greater than the wisdom of man. You need the wisdom of eternity, the wisdom of creation, the wisdom of God. The only source for that wisdom is God. Do not be fooled into thinking that you have the answer. Other people's lives are not playgrounds where you can test out your wisdom.

Point Them to Jesus. You must "preach Christ crucified." To get any lasting solution, they must have a personal relationship with the Lord. Nothing we do or say will be of any help apart from the Lord. The situation in which a suicidal person finds himself may be the result of a life apart from the Lord. The Lord may have brought him to the end of himself so he would trust Him for salvation. The solution to his situation lies in getting things right with the Lord. If he is already saved, then maybe he needs to renew his relationship with the Lord.

Give Them the Word of God. Give them a verse on which to lean. Remember Hebrews 4:12: "For the word of God is quick, and powerful, and sharper than any twoedged sword, piercing even to the dividing asunder of soul and spirit...and is a discerner of the thoughts and intents of the heart." Nothing you can give them can take the place of the Bible.

Purchase a good concordance to help you in looking up verses. Read your Bible daily, so you become familiar with Bible truth. It is the Word that convicts and convinces the heart. It is the Bible that gives assurance, not only for the dying but for the living. "So then faith cometh by hearing, and hearing by the word of God" (Rom. 10:17).

It is not our arguments that will win them over; it is the Bible. We cannot argue them into believing the Bible, nor can we force them to accept it as true. Only the Lord can do those things. It is our job to give them the Word of God, but it is the Holy Spirit's job to help them believe it.

Pray With Them. You usually find a suicidal person will not be on praying terms with the Lord. If he does pray, he probably does not expect to receive anything. He does not trust his own prayers to accomplish much. Do not shortchange the benefits of prayer. Prayer has calmed many a frazzled nerve. In order for your prayer to be more than just words, you yourself must be a màn or woman of prayer. No one can fool the Lord with a false attitude of prayer.

Give Them Your Ear Before You Give Them Your Mouth. Do not give advice hastily, no matter how sound you think it may be. They may need a shoulder to cry on for awhile before you give them your words of encouragement.

Many times we get in a hurry to give our advice. When the answer is hasty, it seems insincere. You will appear as if you really do not understand the true scope of reality if you are too quick to give an answer. Hear them out. Earn the right to be heard by being a good listener; then give them the Word of God.

Bring Them to Your Pastor. The need is a spiritual need. Take them to a spiritual man for counsel. An unsaved man does not understand spiritual truth. The pastors are the counselors for the day in which we live. This is not to say that godly people cannot help, but those in trouble need a good relationship not only with God but also with God's man. Do not just recommend going to your pastor; make appointments and take them to him.

If you do not attend a good church, now would be a good time to start. If you are not in church, your suggestions will seem insincere.

Be Their Friend. People are tired of others' taking advantage of them. We live in a world run by covetousness, fueled by selfishness, and headed to Hell. As Christians, we are to be different. We are not offering others a gimmick to get them into church but a sound solution to help them.

Many do not have one true friend. They are starving for someone to befriend them and to love them. Proverbs 17:17 tells us, "A friend loveth at all times." Christians ought to be the best friends the needy ever had. We ought to be the world's best examples of true, heartfelt compassion. We ought to love others as the Lord loves us.

Try to Help Them Get Their Eyes Off Themselves. As long as they keep their eyes on themselves, they will continue down this long hill of despair. Where they cast their eyes will determine which direction they are going and from which direction their help and hope will come.

"I will lift up mine eyes unto the hills, from whence cometh my help.

"My help cometh from the LORD, which made heaven and earth."—Ps. 121:1, 2.

Get them involved with a ministry. Help them serve the Lord. You may have to get involved with them in order to get them involved. This will require sacrificing of your time and effort, but it will allow you to help them.

Do Not Quit. Often it may seem as if nothing we do works. Everything we offer may be rejected. It may seem as if we are speaking to deaf ears, but we shouldn't quit. It was a long process that brought the suicidal person to this point; it may be a long process to get him out. If there ever is a time your friendship is needed, it is when a person is contemplating suicide.

CONCLUSION

Suicide is a major problem in our world today. It is not a new problem, nor is it insoluble. The Lord has the answer for what we are facing. He can fix a broken heart, dry a tear-stained cheek, and give a glimmer of hope in an otherwise dark world. He can help a devastated loved one. He can help you if you are called upon to be a friend to a suicidal person. He cares more, knows more and can do more than you, but He may want to use you in this way. Trust Him for the solution and the results.

Suicide is a major issue, but our Lord is bigger than the issue. If you are considering suicide as a viable option to your dilemma, think again. Your inability to see another option does not mean one does not exist. Jesus can bring a new beginning to a seemingly devastated life. Let the Lord help you; only then will you find life's purpose.

If you are facing a guilt-ridden life as the result of a loved one's suicide, do not lose hope. Just as Jesus has comfort for the suicidal, He has comfort for those with broken hearts. Come to Him and His Word and find peace for your soul. Come to Jesus, and you will find Him to be a Friend that sticks closer than a brother. There is hope for the suicidal; there is hope for the suicide's grieving loved ones.

For a complete list of books available from the Sword of the Lord, write to Sword of the Lord Publishers, P. O. Box 1099, Murfreesboro, Tennessee 37133.

(800) 251-4100
(615) 893-6700
FAX (615) 848-6943
e-mail: booksales@swordofthelord.com